Strict

Vegetarian

Cookbook

by:
Lorine Tadej

Published by:
M M I Press
Harrisville, New Hampshire

ISBN 0-912145-01-3 Comb
ISBN 0-912145-02-1 Paper

Library of Congress Catalog Card Number 84-61271
Copyright—1984 by Lorine I. Tadej

Cover Photo Credit:
L. Willinger/Shostal Assoc.

TABLE OF CONTENTS

WHY BE A STRICT VEGETARIAN?

Please read the information at the beginning of this book, before using the recipes. It will help you to maintain your good health or restore health, if you have lost it.

God wants you to be happy and healthy and has provided the essentials.

Dear Friend:

These recipes were compiled or invented or adapted with loving care. Please forgive the human errors.

I enclose a prayer for good health.

Food should look good, taste good and be good.

Who but God could have planned so perfectly in His diet for His people?

"In grains, fruits, nuts are to be found all the food elements that we need."   Counsels on Diet and Foods p. 92

"Grains, fruits, nuts and vegetables constitute the diet chosen for us by our Creator. These foods, prepared in as simple and natural a manner as possible, are the most healthful and nourishing."
                                        Ministry of Healing p. 296

"Five hours at least should elapse between each meal and always bear in mind that if you would give it a trial, you would find that two meals are better than three."

"The first education children should receive from the mother in infancy should be in regard to their physical health. They should be allowed only plain food, of that quality that would preserve to them the best condition of health, and that should be partaken of only at regular periods, not oftener than three times a day, and two meals would be better than three."
                            Counsels on Diet and Foods p. 228-229

"Life is a gift of God. Our bodies have been given us to use in God's service and He desires that we shall care for and appreciate them. Our bodies must be kept in the best possible condition physically, and under the most spiritual influences, in order that we may make the best use of our talents."   Counsels on Health p. 41

"The things of nature are God's blessings, provided to give health to body, mind and soul."   Counsels on Health p. 169

"Those who accustom themselves to proper exercise in the open air, will generally have a good and vigorous circulation. More people die for want of exercise than through overfatigue; very many more rust out than wear out."   Counsels on Health p. 173

"Many a mother sets a table that is a snare to her family . . . The mother should study to set a simple yet nutritious diet before her family." Counsels on Diet and Foods p. 236

"Our sisters often do not know how to cook . . . It is your duty to teach your daughters to cook." Counsels on Health p. 144

"Some of you send your daughters, who have nearly grown to womanhood, to school to learn the sciences before they know how to cook, when this should be made of the first importance."
Counsels on Health p. 149

"Food should be prepared with simplicity, yet with a nicety which will invite the appetite ... Let all who sit down at your table see upon it well-cooked, hygenic, palatable food. Eat regularly, and eat only food that is free from grease..."Counsels on Diet and Foods p. 354

"Grains and fruits prepared free from grease, and in as natural a condition as possible, should be the food for the tables of all who claim to be preparing for translation to heaven."
Counsels on Diet and Foods p. 355

(Webster defines 'grease' as an oily matter . . .)

"The free use of sugar in any form tends to clog the system and is not infrequently a cause of disease."
Counsels on Diet and Foods p. 197

"The less of sweet foods that are eaten, the better; these cause disturbances in the stomach and produces impatience and irritability in those who accustom themselves to their use."
Counsels on Diet and Foods p. 321

"God will work wonders for us if we will in faith cooperate with Him. Let us, then, pursue a sensible course, that our efforts may be blessed of Heaven, and crowned with success." Counsels on Health p. 172

Why should we eat so simply? Why should food be eaten in its original form as much as possible? Why eliminate free fats? Why eliminate sugar? Why whole grains? Why avoid refined proteins?

There is really only one reason and it is very simple. God's diet for man. Do you believe God knows what He is doing? Does He balance proteins, fats, sugars, starches, vitamins, minerals, fiber content, etc., in His food?

vegetables and grains every day. Only food that is eaten feeds the body, so make your food tasty and attractive to your family. A stew or soup or salad can be a meal. Serve it with whole grain bread.

11. What about salt?

Taste your combined ingredients BEFORE adding salt. Always start with half the amount suggested in the recipe. If you need any, it takes less if the salt can be added to already hot food. Adding a little lemon juice may make salt unnecessary.

Non-Irritating Herbs

Anise seed
Basil
Bay leaf
Caraway
Celery seed
Coriander
Cumin
Dill seed
Fennel seed
Garlic
Mace
Marjoram
Mint
Onion
Oregano
Paprika
Parsley
Poppy seed
Rosemary
Saffron
Sage
Sesame seed
Tarragon
Thyme
Turmeric

Try these in small amounts until you see how your family likes them.

Introduction

This information will help you to reach your ideal weight and maintain it, as long as you live.

Adam and Eve were an ideal weight because they ate food, as God gave it to them, in a natural state.

You can follow God's food plan today and you will be amazed, as I was, at how easily you can reach and keep *your* perfect weight.

Tell your family that you do not want to hear the word *diet*. To start with; a diet is a temporary weight loss plan and this program is for life.

After I had lost about 25 or 30 pounds, the praise did help. Fatties need support in words and actions. Thanks so much to those who really helped!

As a fatty, I know all the tricks and deceptions.

As soon as I was alone, I started to eat. I also ate in the night because no one was watching. I hid junk food in my own dresser drawers.

All of this helped my meals to seem a sensible size.

Until I had fully accepted the present plan for my life, I just got very busy at the times food would be the greatest temptation. I have never been hungry once on this program.

Getting every bit of junk food out of the house helped a lot and I have never felt deprived.

Please write if I can help in any way. We *all* need help sometimes.

I want everyone who reads these pages to have a "Newstart."

N   nutrition
E   exercise
W   water
S   sunshine
T   temperance
A   air
R   rest
T   trust in God

I have written about each of these factors to show how they have helped me to reach my ideal weight and have maximum health.

Nutrition

I, Lorine Tadej, challenge you to follow this plan for 30 days and then to follow it all of your days.

You can do anything for one month, can't you, dear friend?

One doctor has said, "There are built-in safety factors in the natural food that God provided for us, that prevent us from becoming obese. On a natural diet where no sugar or visible fats of any kind are added to the diet, obese patients will lose weight, even though they are eating all that they want."

Fruits and vegetables do not digest at the same rate, so it is best to have 2 vegetable meals and 1 fruit meal or 2 fruit meals and 1 vegetable meal.

Use natural, unrefined foods *only* and *always*.

Do not allow between meals eating ever.

Have regular meals 5 to 5½ hours apart 7 days a week. Very rarely let anything interfere with this plan, even though well-meaning friends and relatives will sometimes make it difficult.

Do not have any sugar, mayonnaise, margarine or other refined foods in the house.

Exclude all so-called foods that are high in calories with minimal or no nutrition.

Eat whole grain products (bread or cereal) at every meal because they are low in calories but high in fiber and food value.

It will take only a few minutes to count the fresh vegetables in your market. In January, I found 55 different ones. There were 21 fresh fruits even in midwinter.

There are about 12 grains and an equal number of legumes plus seeds and nuts so your food program has fantastic possibilities.

Here are the 3 rules that can help you attain an ideal weight.

1) Eat food as close to the way it grows as possible.
2) Have a wide variety over a week's time.
3) Eat enough food to maintain *your* correct weight at *your* exercise level.

Keep your salt intake low, so start with ½ the amount a recipe calls for. Use fresh lemon juice and learn to use herbs for seasoning. Use small amounts of herbs until you decide on the ones you and your family like and how much.

The ten worst junk foods should never waste your money. They are:

1) All soft drinks
2) White flour products
3) Sweet rolls and pastry
4) Candy
5) Fruit drinks
6) Heavily salted snacks
7) Fats such as cooking oils, mayonnaise, margarine, shortenings, butter, salad dressings and cheese.
8) Potato chips (a baked potato is an excellent food, about 80-90 calories). One potato made into french fries is 274 calories and one potato made into chips is 565 calories and has almost *no* nutrients.
9) Frozen desserts, some of which have no food at all but are just chemicals.
10) Imitation foods such as dairy substitutes and instant meals.

The average American eats over 100 pounds of refined sugar a year but sugar addicts will never admit it, any more than an alcoholic will admit he drinks too much. A recovering alcoholic can never have even one drink. An ex-smoker cannot have one cigarette and fatties or ex-fatties should not have any refined sugars, chocolate, or visible (free) fats. Honey is at least 80% sugar, by the way.

This section has menus-suggestions-meanings.

1) Main meals should be in the morning or at noon, if at all possible.
2) We have had our vegetables, entree, and salad at 7 a.m. for many years. Our five children grew up this way and still follow the plan or at least have a generous morning meal.
3) When you combine a grain and legume, you have the essential amino acids or protein. It is easier to get too much protein than too little, since nearly all natural food has some protein.
4) Vegetable relishes are raw vegetables such as carrot and celery sticks, cauliflower, green peppers, radishes, onions, zucchini, cucumbers, turnips, kohlrabi, etc. You can use these vegetables, in season, every day, if you wish, since they are low in calories, filling, and high in nutrients.

5) Have a variety of foods over a week's time.
6) The largest meal should include vegetables (raw and cooked), a main dish, and whole grain bread.
7) The breakfast meal should have 2 or 3 fruits (separate or combined), whole grain cereal, and/or bread.
8) The third meal can be fruit and bread or vegetable soup or salad and bread.
9) All breads and cereals should be whole grain and a combination of grains is better than just wheat.
10) Chewy food takes longer to eat, so gives your appestat a chance to work.
11) Cook vegetables a short time and steaming is the best method. Do not peel potatoes and carrots.
12) Have different kinds of bread for taste and health.
13) Vary grains, legumes, and nuts.
14) Do not settle for 3 or 4 vegetables and fruits. Use many varieties, so you do not feel limited.

All of the recipes for the following menus are in this cookbook.

BREAD
(Dough Hook Method)

Put in the bowl:

5	c. hot water	⅓	c. peanut oil or 1 avocado
1	c. apple or pear sauce	2	T. salt
1	c. dopep or soy flour	3	T. dry yeast

Add about 16 cups whole grain flour. Beat 10 minutes. Put in pans and let rise until double in size. Bake at 350 degrees until done.

BREAD
(Regular Method)

Put in largest electric mixer bowl:

5	c. hot water	⅓	c. peanut oil or 1 avocado
1	c. apple or pear sauce	2	T. salt
1	c. dopep or soy flour	3	T. dry yeast
10	c. whole grain flour		

Mix these ingredients at least 10 minutes. Add enough more flour to kneading consistency and knead 10 minutes. Let dough rise until double in size. Punch down and form into loaves. Let rise until double in size and bake at 350 degrees until done.

Vegetable Meal Menus

Third Meal Menus

Vegetable soups or salads or fruits plus bread. You can use any salads in the book or have 2 or 3 fruits with bread and/or cereal. Following are a list of soups:

Sack Lunches

Fruits

You are not limited to oranges, apples or bananas. Try grapes, melons, fruits canned in juice, grapefruit slices, berries, etc. Score citrus fruits for easy peeling.

Raw Vegetables

Not only carrots and celery but radishes, kholrabi, zucchini, turnips green peppers, cauliflower, cherry tomatoes, broccoli or cucumbers.

Sandwiches

Use a variety of whole grain bread, rolls, and crackers.

Fillings

Use peanut butter with sugarless jams or raisins or banana slices. There are numerous patties or vegetarian burgers or mash any legume (beans). Add sprouts and/or tomatoes, onions, avocadoes, diced celery, spinach leaves.

Cereals

Combine home-made granola or brown rice, barley, oat groats with fruits such as applesauce or any blended fruit canned in juice or berries canned or frozen without sugar or dried fruit soaked overnight in juice.

Cookies

Here is a Home Exercise Program given to me at a Pain Control Center:

I) Position: Backlying, knees flexed, feet flat on the floor.

1. **PELVIC TILT:** Flatten low back. Hold for a count of 3. Release.

   Maintain pelvic tilt in all of the following exercises:

2. **PARTIAL SIT UP:** Chin to chest, raise head, reach hands to top of knees. Lower hands, lower head, release chin.

3. **ELBOWS TO KNEE:** Place hands on shoulders. Take elbow to opposite knee. This may be done with the head on the floor initially. Progress to raising head.

4. **STRAIGHT LEG RAISE:** Flex the opposite knee. Tighten the thigh muscles of the straight leg. Raise leg slowly and lower slowly. Maintain pelvic tilt throughout.

5. **HIP AND KNEE ROLL:** Press knees together. Roll knees to one side, raise up to mid-line, roll to the opposite side. Maintain pelvic tilt throughout.

6. **8-COUNT ARM EXERCISE:** 1-up, 2-above head, 3-up, 4-out to side, 5-up, 6-touch opposite shoulders, 7-up, 8-arms to side.

II) Position: Sidelying.

1. **STRAIGHT LEG RAISING:** Be sure that leg is in line with trunk, the underneath knee is flexed.

III) Position: Long-sitting, leaning up against a wall, progress to free sitting.

1. **QUADRICEPS SET:** Tighten thigh muscles, press knees down into floor, pull toes up towards the ceiling. Hold strongly for a count of 5, release. Repeat with the opposite leg.

2. **HAMSTRING STRETCH:** One knee flexed one knee straight. Hold flexed knee with one hand. Reach the other hand towards the toes of the straight leg, hold for a count of 5, release. Repeat with the opposite leg.

3. **TRUNK FORWARD FLEXION:** Separate feet as wide apart as is comfortable, rotate feet outwards. Place hands

on the insides of the knees. Flex elbows to bring trunk forwards. Back should be straight throughout movement. Progress to free sitting (away from wall) reaching hands towards toes.

IV) Position: Hands and knees, hands placed directly beneath shoulders. Maintain a right angle at all joints.

1. **MAD CAT:** Arch low back into pelvic tilt position, pulling in with the abdominal muscles, tuck buttocks under so back is rounded. Reverse movement until back is flat.

2. **ROCKING:** Pelvic tilt, round low back, sit back on heels, keep head low. Maintain straight arms throughout. Return to starting position.

3. **REACHING AROUND FROM SIDE TO SIDE:** Touch foot with hand of same side, turn head to look at foot. Repeat to opposite side.

4. **TRUNK TWIST:** Reach hand under arch to touch opposite shoulder, bring hand out and straighten outwards and upwards to the same side. Turn head to watch hand throughout movement. Repeat opposite side.

V) Position: Sitting on the front half of a straight back chair.

1. **FORWARD BENDING:** With knees apart, curl trunk forward as you breathe out, arms should be relaxed and forwards. Raise trunk as you breathe in.

2. **GLIDING:** Keeping arms out to the side and in line with the trunk, bend slowly from side to side.

3. **SHOULDER ROLLING:** Circle shoulders a) forwards b) backwards.

4. **NECK MOVEMENTS:** Maintain upright posture of head and shoulders throughout.
   i.) forwards and backwards
   ii.) side to side
   iii.) ear to shoulder

VI) Position: Standing

1. **PELVIC TILT:** Lean back against a wall. Place the heel of one foot against the wall also, place the other foot in front in a normal walking pace position.

Slide back down wall until the low back is in contact with the wall. The knees will have to be flexed to maintain this position. Hold pelvic tilt. Take one step away from the wall, return back to the wall to see if you have maintained the pelvic tilt.

2. **SIDE STRETCH:** Stand alongside wall with feet together, extend arm out sideways to touch wall. Lean inwards towards wall.

3. **ARM CIRCLES:** Stand with arms out sideways. Rotate arms in widening circles a) forwards b) backwards.

VII) Position: Walking.
1. **TOE WALK**
2. **HEEL WALK**
3. **STEP-SQUAT-STAND:**
   i.) Take normal size step
   ii.) Flex knees
   iii.) Straighten knees

   Progress by flexing knees more during part ii.) of the exercise.

Water

Life itself depends on water and over one-half of your own body is water.

You lose about 2 to 2½ quarts of water each day and for good health you must take in at least this much through food eaten and water drunk.

Thirst is not always a reliable guide to your need for water, so drink even if you are not thirsty. An adult needs 8 to 10 glasses of water per day.

If you need to learn to drink enough, fill a 2 quart pitcher full of water in the morning. Drink from this pitcher and it should be empty at the end of the day.

Drinking a lot of water increases your endurance to resist disease and promotes better circulation of your lifeblood.

Do not drink with meals, as it delays digestion.

Water is the only drink you ever need.

Use water freely on the outside also. A daily bath or shower is essential to remove body wastes.

Relaxing by a stream, lake, or the ocean promotes health.

Thank God for the marvelous life-giving, health-promoting gift of water.

An abundance is a necessity for weight control and drink it between meals. Drink at least ½ hour before meals and 1 hour after eating.

Sunshine

"One of the most healing agents of nature is sunshine," comments one author.

Through its abuse, however, 220,000 persons every year in the United States discover they have skin cancer. Five thousand of these Americans die each year, as a result of too much solar radiation.

The proper amount of sun gives you Vitamin D, kills harmful bacteria and virus, lowers chelesterol and triglyceride levels, increases liver function and promotes healing of wounds.

That lovely sunshine also helps your heart, lungs, and blood vessels to do their work efficiently.

Sunshine lowers blood pressure, helps you resist disease, and it aids your metabolism in burning up fat cells quickly.

Get outdoors regardless of the weather, because you get the benefit of ultaviolet rays, even on a rainy or snowy day.

When at all possible, sunbathe outdoors before 10 a.m. or after 3 p.m. in the Snowbelt and before 9 a.m. or after 4 p.m. in the Sunbelt. There are fluorescent sunlamps available for indoor sunbathing but they are second best and use them with the utmost caution.

It has been learned through research that a person on a low fat diet can take more sun rays without burning.

Let us be grateful for and take advantage of God's lifegiving, health-producing power that He has given us in sunlight.

Temperance

I am enclosing here some quotations from an author who wrote hundreds of pages on temperance and also lectured widely on this subject. I am in agreement with the statements and know these principles will help you in reaching and maintaining *your* ideal weight.

"In order to preserve health, temperance in all things is necessary-temperance in labor, temperance in eating and drinking."
Counsels on Diet and Foods, p. 23
Ellen G. White

"The only safe course is to touch not, taste not, handle not, tea, coffee, wines, tobacco, opium, and alcoholic drinks."
Counsels on Diet and Foods, p. 428
Ellen White

"Temperance reformers have a work to do in educating the people in these lines. Teach them that health, character, and even life, are endangered by the use of stimulants, which excite the exhausted energies to unnatural, spasmodic action."
Counsels on Diet and Foods, p. 429-30
Ellen G. White

"Indulgence of appetite is the greatest cause of physical and mental debility, and lies at the foundation of the feebleness which is apparent everywhere." **Temperance,** p. 15
Ellen G. White

"When the appetite for spiritous liquor is indulged . . . reason is paralyzed." **Temperance,** p. 23
Ellen G. White

"Tobacco, in whatever form it is used, tells upon the constitution. It is a slow poison. It affects the brain and benumbs the sensibilities..."
Temperance, p. 55
Ellen G. White

"Those who engaged in running the race to obtain that laurel which was considered a special honor, were temperate in all things, so that their muscles, their brains, and every part of them, might be in the very best condition to run." **Counsels on Health,** p. 46-7
Ellen G. White

"It is a great thing to insure health by placing ourselves in right relations to the laws of life." **Counsels on Health, p. 49**
Ellen G. White

"The harmonious, healthy action of all the powers of body and mind results in happiness; the more elevated and refined the powers, the more pure and unalloyed the happiness." **Counsels on Health, p. 51**
Ellen G. White

"Far too much sugar is ordinarily used in food. Cakes, sweet puddings, pastries, jellies, jams, are active causes of indigestion." **Counsels on Diet and Foods, p.113**
Ellen G. White

"The less that condiments and desserts are placed upon our tables, the better it will be for all who partake of the food." **Counsels on Diet and Foods, p. 113**
Ellen G. White

"The free use of sugar in any form tends to clog the system, and is not unfrequently a cause of disease." **Counsels on Diet and Foods, p.197**
Ellen G. White

"All should be acquainted with the special value of fruits and vegetables fresh from the orchard and garden." **Counsels on Diet and Foods, p. 321**
Ellen G. White

"Show a purity of taste, appetite, and habits that bears comparison with Daniel's. God will reward you with calm nerves, a clear brain, and unimpaired judgement, keen perceptions." **Messages to Young People, p. 244**
Ellen G. White

Temperance enters into every area of our lives. The dictionary defines it as moderation-a desired virtue-and as self control and calmness.

Total abstinence is essential in most areas because of the addiction.

Most of us want clear minds and healthy bodies, so let us rid ourselves of harmful chemicals in food and drink and drugs.

Air

A free abundance of fresh air is a blessing available to all.

Many die because they deny themselves fresh air to keep their health or restore diseased bodies.

Sick people especially need fresh air at all times.

Let fresh air into your homes daily and keep windows open at night regardless of the weather.

One author writes:

"In order to have good blood, we must breathe well. Full, deep inspirations of pure air which fill the lungs with oxygen, purify the blood. They impart to it a bright color, and send it, a life-giving current, to every part of the body. A good respiration soothes the nerves; it stimulates the appetite, and renders digestion more perfect; and it induces sound, refreshing sleep."

Counsels on Health, p. 59
Ellen G. White

"Air, air, the precious boon of heaven, which all may have, will bless you with its invigorating influence, if you will not refuse it entrance. Welcome it, cultivate a love for it, and it will prove a precious soother of the nerves. Air must be in constant circulation to be kept pure. The influence of pure fresh air is to cause the blood to circulate healthfully through the system. It refreshes the body, and tends to render it strong and healthy, while at the same time its influence is decidedly felt upon the mind, inparting a degree of composure and serenity. It excites the appetite, and renders the digestion of food more perfect, and induces sound and sweet sleep."

Counsels on Health, p. 60
Ellen G. White

"Life in the open air is good for body and mind. It is God's medicine for the restoration of health. Pure air, good water, sunshine, the beautiful surroundings of nature-these are His means for restoring the sick to health in natural ways. To the sick it is worth more than silver or gold to lie in the sunshine or in the shade of the trees."

Counsels on Health, p. 166
Ellen G. White

Deep breathing helps you to relax and can help you to go to sleep. Fresh air is vital to good health and activates your metabolism. Slim bodies are more likely to be healthy ones.

Rest

The human body and mind must have rest and a change of pace to function properly.

A regular time to go to bed and a regular time to get up should be followed every day of the week. It is vital to good health and has a definite effect on weight control.

The amount of sleep needed is not the same for each person but regularity *is* for everyone.

While we sleep our minds and bodies are going through a restorative process, which they need.

People deprived of rest can become both physically and mentally ill.

Never eat later then 4 hours before retiring.

Deep breathing and light exercise just before bedtime promotes relaxation to help you get to sleep and a lukewarm soak in a tub may help also.

Learn techniques to relax your body and mind completely.

People who engage in mostly "sit-down" jobs need physical exercise for a change and to maintain health.

Recreation should be just that-time and activity which will recreate mental, physical, and spiritual processes.

One author has made this suggestion:

"Let several families living in a city or village unite and leave the occupations which have taxed them physically and mentally, and make an excursion into the country, to the side of a fine lake, or to a nice grove, where the scenery of nature is beautiful. They should provide themselves with plain, hygienic food, the very best fruits and grains, and spread their table under the shade of some tree, or under the canopy of heaven. The ride, the exercise, and the scenery, will quicken the appetite, and they can enjoy a repast which kings might envy.

"On such occasions parents and children should feel free from care, labor, and perplexity. Parents should become children with their children, making everything as pleasant for them as possible. Let the whole day be given to recreation. Exercise in the open air, for those whose employment has been within doors and sedentary, will be beneficial to health. All who can, should feel it a duty to pursue this course. Nothing will be lost, but much gained. They can return to their occupations with new life and new courage to engage in their labor with zeal, and they are better prepared to resist disease."   **Counsels on Health,** p. 195-6
Ellen G. White

Happy Dreams!

Trust

Belief in your God-given abilities will be a tremendous aid in reaching and maintaining your goal of maximum health.

Learn to relax completely. It will take time but it is well worth the effort to learn to relax physically and mentally.

The best method I have found is to concentrate on one area, such as the left hand, until it is totally limp and then move on, until your entire body is void of all tension.

Twenty-five things that will help you to have a peaceful, productive life are:

1) Get plenty of exercise.
2) Get enough rest for your needs.
3) Eat regular, natural food meals always-no sugar.
4) Do the things you know are right and good.
5) Find an outlet for your creative abilities in a hobby or recreation.
6) Do something nice for somone *often*.
7) Stop to smell the roses, listen to a child, and touch the elderly.
8) Smile-smile-smile.
9) Listen-really listen-for the ticking of a clock, bird songs, falling rain, or your own breathing.
10) Plan some idle time every day.
11) Read something that requires concentration.
12) Have a place to be alone.
13) Avoid people who irritate you, whenever possible.
14) Plan vacations for leisure.
15) Do something to give yourself a better life.
16) Live by months and years instead of minutes and seconds.
17) Concentrate on one objective at a time.
18) Keep happy thoughts.
19) Let a clear conscience be your tranquilizer.
20) Be gracious about others' shortcomings but critical of your own.
21) Take deep breaths of fresh air several times a day.
22) Have adequate clothing and bedding, so your entire body is warm day and night, indoors and outdoors.
23) Take a daily bath or shower.
24) Drink 8-10 glasses of water daily.
25) Pray.

Summary

Here are some helpers on the way to the correct size *you*. The results are guaranteed.

1) Get adequate rest.
2) Exercise daily.
3) Get plenty of fresh air and sunshine.
4) Make eating and food preparation a secondary part of your life.
5) Be sure your food looks good, tastes good, and is good nutritionally.
6) Set a good example and a silent one, unless you are asked for help.
7) Eat regularly so you do not get hungry.
8) Eat happily.
9) Put all of the food to be eaten at the meal on your plate at one time.
10) *No* second helpings.
11) Take smaller portions of the higher calorie foods.
12) Limit even nutritious desserts to once or twice a week.
13) Eat slowly.
14) Learn to say, "No, thank you," sweetly, and mean it.
15) Weigh only *once a week* and your goal is one pound each week. Never have a goal of 5 pounds or 25 pounds or 50 pounds over any length of time. Your goal is one pound in seven days and no panic if you don't lose it.
16) Many will find help in a prayer before each meal asking for wisdom and self control.
17) Breakfast like a king, lunch like a queen, and eat a pauper's supper.
18) Have your three meals 5 to 5½ hours apart.
19) A graph for 6 to 12 months, on which to chart your progress will help you.
20) Many are benefited by group therapy, so join up with your friends who need a weight change also.
21) *Never never never* eat between meals.
22) Drink plain water only and lots of it between meals.
23) No coffee, tea, alcohol, or soft drinks *ever*.
24) Make menus for at least one week and preferably for one month. In this book there are 35 days of menus.

25) Eat abundantly of fruits and vegetables prepared simply but tastefully.

26) Use whole grains every meal.

"Pure air, sunlight, abstemiousness, rest, exercise, proper diet, the use of water, trust in divine power-these are the true remedies. Every person should have a knowledge of nature's remedial agencies and how to apply them." **Counsels on Health,** p. 90
Ellen G. White

"So closely is health related to our happiness, that we cannot have the latter without the former. A practical knowledge of the science of human life is necessary in order to glorify God in our bodies. It is therefore of the highest importance, that among the studies selected for childhood, physiology should occupy the first place. How few know anything about the structure and functions of their own bodies, and of nature's laws! Many are drifting about without compass or anchor; and what is more, they are not interested to learn how to keep their bodies in a healthy condition, and prevent disease." **Counsels on Health,** p. 38
Ellen G. White

"Another precious blessing is proper exercise. There are many indolent, inactive ones who are disinclined to physical labor or exercise because it wearies them. Why does it weary them? The reason why they become weary is that they do not strengthen their muscles by exercise, therefore they feel the least exertion."
Counsels on Health, p. 52
Ellen G. White

"When the weather will permit, all who can possibly do so ought to walk in the open air every day, summer and winter."
Counsels on Health, p. 52
Ellen G. White

"Those who are always busy, and go cheerfully about the performance of their daily tasks, are the most happy and healthy."
Counsels on Health, p. 53
Ellen G. White

Remember that Jesus tells us in III John, verse 2:

"Dear Friend, I pray that you may enjoy good health and that all may go well with you." *NIV*

I, Lorine Tadej, desire you to have healthy happiness.

Put the following list where you will read it at the beginning of every day. It may help your "I Choose Power."

"Just for Today"

1) Just for today I will eat 2 or 3 fresh fruits.
2) Just for today I will eat some green and yellow vegetables.
3) Just for today I will eat whole-grain cereals and bread.
4) Just for today I will eat legumes (beans) and no meat.
5) Just for today I will take a long leisurely walk.
6) Just for today I will be thankful-whatever the weather.
7) Just for today I will drink 8 glasses of water.
8) Just for today I will spend 8 relaxed hours in bed.
9) Just for today I will get fresh air day and night.
10) Just for today I will express gratitude to God for at least ten things.

Here are six experiences from friends who have adopted this lifestyle.

Dear Friends,

I'm the type who always gains weight even if I only breathe the food I'm around.

I've tried every so-called organic diet method I could get my hands on. I would not take any drugs.

Then I heard more and more about this diet of eating all foods in the unrefined state, no oils and no sugars. I bought these foods and stocked our cupboards.

Shortly after this my husband was diagnosed as diabetic.

To my surprise, our doctor recommended this very diet as the best diet for a diabetic.

We both went on the diet and my husband's blood sugar dropped and I lost 30 pounds.

I ate 3 meals a day and felt so good.

As time slipped by, I've slipped now and then, but always feel that old oppressed feeling I'd had in the past come back on me.

I feel better all the time, so the better I feel the worse I feel when I slip off the diet.

I feel my diet is like my relationship with Christ. If I slip and fall, and I do, I just reach out and get right back on track. The price is too high to allow myself to stay off of it.

Sincerely in Christ,
Shirley Hare

I would like to write this letter to you to tell you how a proper diet has changed my life.

My former meals consisted of whatever was to my liking. I loved meat, a good cup of coffee and white bread with lots of butter on it. I did not care for vegetables.

I began to have trouble with my stomach and after going from doctor to doctor and taking hundreds of pills, I finally ended up in the hospital, where I had a major operation for diverticulitis. After recovering from the operation I was sent home. I still had digestive problems, so I returned to the hospital where the doctors discovered I also had ulcerated colitis. For this I had to take treatments for months.

Fortunately, I found someone who could tell me what had caused my problems and what to do to overcome such conditions as diverticulitis and colitis. It was all in the food that I had been eating.

My diet was changed to WHOLE WHEAT BREAD, GRAINS, VEGETABLES and such things as the Good Lord had intended for our diet in the first place. No coffee, tea or oils, and the best part is that you learn to enjoy and like this type of a diet.

April 1982 I was 78 years old and am feeling fine. I am able to do several hours of yard work daily. If only I had started this diet or I should say type of eating when I was fifty years or younger, I would have saved myself many dollars and a lot of suffering.

I would like to recommend this method of foods to everyone, and would suggest that they don't wait until they are sick but start when they are young and healthy.

Sincerely,

Ernest C. Comer

When I went on this lifestyle which included exercise in the fresh air, sunshine, only sugar as found in natural foods like dates, raisins, etc., no free fats and trust in my Heavenly Father. I lost 20 pounds immediately and then gained gradually back until I now weigh the recommended weight for my height and frame which is easily held at this level. My blood pressure came down to 127/78. I feel good, enjoy good health, praise God, I give Him all the praise.

Allen Field

I will soon be seventy-one years old. I weighed two hundred pounds by the age of nine. I had headaches often all my life. At thirty-six years I weighed 285 lbs. I had problems if I ate much raw food of any kind.

I would be running to the toilet several times at night plus several times during the day.

Then about five years ago I started having ulcers on my feet. It would take weeks to get them healed up and then before long they would come again.

Finally, last Sept. I lost my right leg because of hardening of the arteries. When I came home from the hospital eight months ago I started eating the way God intended us to eat in the beginning.

We eat no refined food, no sugar, no free fats, no concentrated proteins, very little salt.

I seldom have headaches any more. I eat lots of raw fruits and vegetables with no bowel problems. I weigh 160 lbs. and eat all I want without gaining.

I haven't had any ulcers on my left foot for eight whole months. I thank the Lord for what He has done for me. He keeps His promises when we honor Him by obeying His word.

Herbert Young

"Always Over Weight"

All my life I've had to fight a weight problem. I've tried every diet that I ever heard about. Sometimes I would lose a few pounds-but I always gained it back, and more too. I always had to buy ugly clothes, mu mu type and such. I was always the biggest one in my family.

When my mother was put in a nursing home close to where I live I would spend three to four days a week with her. There was a ramp I had to climb three floors up. I started losing weight so I decided to take advantage of it. I put myself on a diet of my own. I gave up oils of every kind and all sugar and salt.

I exercised every morning for about 20 minutes and I rode my exercise bike for 5 miles each morning. I am up to 10 miles a day now.

Now I am the thinnest one in my family and I am very happy. I have a heart problem which is very much improved. I can buy nice clothes, no more mu mu's.

I think most important is that I asked God's help and He answered my prayer.

I have lost 65 pounds.

Thank you Jesus,

Marjorie Starr

Mildred Haubry told her story to me, Lorine Tadej, and I want to share some of her experiences with you.

Mildred has been a non-meat eater for 30 years but a totally natural foods eater only a little over a year at this writing.

She had been a diabetic for nineteen years and on 50 units of insulin daily for ten years.

Mildred had been very ill and extremely depressed for 13 years, during which time she took tranquilizers contiuously. The drugs, depression and other illnesses turned her into a recluse.

Five years ago Mildred was nearly blind, as a result of the diabetes.

About 15 months ago, Mildred Haubry listened to a series of taped messages by Dr. Zane Kime. He recommended God's lifestyle in using unrefined foods, no sugar, no free fats, whole grains, legumes, vegetables and fruits, daily exercise suitable to age and ability, sunlight, fresh air, at least 6 to 8 glasses of water for God's healing through His laws of health and happiness.

Mildred had only one direction to move, since she had hit bottom healthwise.

She is now a delightful, vivacious lady.

She has taken *no* insulin and *no* tranquilzers for many months.

She has lost 60 excess pounds without effort and her eyesight has remarkably improved. Her doctor says it is almost unbelievable.

Mildred knows that God answers prayer and gives physical, mental and spiritual health. She, also, recently had some special assistance from her guardian angel in a time of need.

If you do not wish to use McKay's Chicken- or Beef- seasonings, you can make your own by the following recipe and use it wherever McKays is called for in recipes.

CHICKEN—STYLE SEASONING

Mix Well:

1/2	c. lightly toasted fine cornmeal	1/2	c. food yeast flakes
1	tsp. each garlic powder onion powder sage thyme	1/2	tsp. turmeric
		1	Tblsp. each celery salt vegesal dried parsley leaves

If you do not want to use mushrooms, they are optional in *most* recipes.

I use Pam as a spray on pans that do not have a non-stick surface, since it contains lecithin, is convenient to use, and is low calorie.

Cinnamon is a slightly irritating spice. If it bothers your stomach, you can use coriander or cardamon instead or combine them.

Soy sauce is a fermented substance, but two items that take the place of soy sauce in all recipes are Dr. Bronner's "Balanced Soya-Mineral Bullion" or Bragg's "Liquid Aminos." Both of these are usually found in health food stores or cooperative stores.

We do want our food to taste good, so our families will eat it. Be sure to ask God to help you to enjoy *His* program for a healthful lifestyle.

Our protein should be 10% of our caloric intake. Research has shown that all Americans get more protein than needed and too much of it can lower resistance to disease, increase the aging process, decrease assimilation of needed nutrients and cause much loss of calcium which leads to osteoporosis.

You should have unprocessed proteins for breakfast, when you should eat 1/3 to 1/2 of your daily needed nutrients.

If lunch contains natural protein foods, the evening meal does not need them.

Please remember that fruits and vegetables should always make up the largest part of a meal.

BREADS

Non-Yeast Breads:

ALMOND PIE CRUST

1½	c. ground almonds	2	tsp. water
3	Tbsp. flour	¼	tsp. salt

Grind nuts in grinder. Mix flour, nut meal and salt; add water and mix well. Press into pie pan.

Bake at 300 degrees for 45 minutes. Use with pie filling.

BOSTON BROWN BREAD

4	c. whole grain flours	1	c. chopped nuts
⅓	c. molasses	1	Tbsp. grated orange rind
1	c. raisins	1	tsp. salt
2	c. water		

Mix; put in a Pam sprayed Pyrex or stainless steel mixing bowl. Steam for 2 hours in a covered kettle.

CASHEW CRACKERS

Blend:

1	c. raw cashews	½	c. hot water
½	tsp. salt		

Add:

1   c. whole wheat flour

Spread thin on a cookie sheet.

Bake at 350 degrees until crisp, at least 30 minutes.

CORN CRACKERS

2	c. cornmeal	1	tsp. salt
1	c. cashew meal (blended)	4	Tbsp. sesame seed
1	c. walnut meal (blended)	1	c. water

Spread very thin on a cookie sheet.

Bake at 250 degrees until very dry.

CORN MUFFINS

Blend:

2	c. soaked soybeans, well drained	8	dates
2	c. hot water	2	tsp. salt
		¼	c. raw oatmeal

Add:

2   c. cornmeal

Fill muffin tins and bake at 400 degrees for 35 minutes.

CORNMEAL RICE CAKES

1	c. cornmeal	1	c. cooked rice
4	Tbsp. soy flour	½	c. ground sunflower seeds
½	tsp. salt	1	c. boiling water

Mix cornmeal, flour and salt. Add boiling water. Mix well until moisture is absorbed. Add rice and sunflower seeds. Mix. Place in mounds on cookie sheet, flatten to about ½ inch thickness.

Bake at 400 degrees for 30 minutes, or until brown.

FRENCH TOAST

Blend and then pour into a shallow dish:

1	c. hot water	6	dates
1	c. apple juice	½	tsp. salt
1	c. raw cashews	¼	c. whole wheat flour

Dip bread slices in the batter and brown slowly on both sides in a nonstick or Pam-sprayed pan.

Top with any fruit or berries hot or cold.

GRANOLA

Mix:

3	c. rolled oats	½	c. wheat germ
1	c. whole wheat flour	½	c. coconut
½	c. cornmeal	½	c. sunflower seeds
½	c. rye flour	½	c. sesame seeds
½	c. millet meal		

Blend and add, then mix well:

1	c. peanut butter	8	dates
6	oz. apple juice conc.	1	tsp. vanilla

Spread on cookie sheets and bake at 250 degrees until dry.

OATMEAL CRACKERS

2	c. nut meal (blended)	1	tsp. salt
1	c. cold water	2	c. quick oatmeal

Spread very thin on a cookie sheet.

Bake at 250 degrees until completely dry and crisp.

SESAME OAT SQUARES

Blend:

1	c. raw cashews	1	c. dates
1	c. hot water		

Add:

1½	c. sesame seeds	½	tsp. salt
¾	c. soy flour	1	tsp. vanilla
1	c. whole wheat flour		

Pat thin and bake until golden brown at 325 degrees.

WAFFLES

⅓	c. cashews	¾	c. whole wheat flour
1	c. water	1	tsp. salt
2½	c. oats	4 to 4½	c. hot water
¾	c. cornmeal		

Blend cashews and 1 cup water first. Then add alternately with the liquefier on, part of hot water (2 to 3 cups) and all the grains and salt. When blended smoothly, pour batter into a large bowl. Add the rest of the water and mix thoroughly.

Spray waffle iron lightly with Pam while it is still cold. Then put on high heat.

Bake waffles in hot waffle iron for 8 to 12 minutes. Even with many batches, you won't have to use any more Pam. Do not peek for at least 8 minutes.

Use 1½ cups batter for each large waffle. These waffles can be frozen and reheated.

Yield: 4 large waffles.

WHOLE WHEAT CRACKERS

4	c. wl. wheat pastry flour	½	c. peanut butter
1	c. water	1	tsp. salt

Mix peanut butter and water. Pour into flour. Roll out thin. Bake at 350 degrees for 20 minutes, or until golden brown.

SOY WAFFLES

Soak overnight:

1   **c. soybeans**

Drain well

Blend thoroughly:

2½	c. warm water	½	c. sunflower seeds
1½	c. rolled oats	½	tsp. salt
	soaked soybeans		

Bake 10-15 minutes in a hot waffle iron. These may be made ahead and reheated.

Yeast Breads:

CORNBREAD

Mix and set aside:

2	Tbsp. yeast	½	applesauce
1	c. hot water		

Mix:

4½	c. hot water	4½	c. cornmeal
½	c. oil or 2 blended	⅔	c. soy flour
	avocados	¾	c. gluten flour
1½	Tbsp. salt		

Add yeast mixture.

Mix all and add 4 to 6 cups whole wheat flour as needed. Knead 10 minutes. Let rise 45 minutes. Punch down. Put in pans and let rise until double in size.

Bake at 350 degrees for 45-60 minutes.

KOLACHES

Combine:

1½	c. flour	1	tsp. salt
2	Tbsp. yeast	1	c. hot water
½	c. applesauce	¼	c. oil or 1 blended avocado

Beat well, Add 1½ to 2 cups more flour. Mix well. Shape bread into about 1½ inch balls and place on cookie sheet. Let rise 15 minutes. Use 2 fingers and make an indentation in each. Put in 1 teaspoon of filling, pressing with spoon slightly. Let rise 15 minutes.

Bake at 400 degrees for 15 to 20 minutes.

Fillings:

A. **Dried fruits and/or nuts**
B. **Vegetables, finely chopped**

MULTI-GRAIN BREAD

Liquefy:

5	c. warm water	¾	c. dates

Add:

4	c. whole wheat flour	2 pkgs. yeast	

Stir and let rise 30 minutes.

Add:

4	Tbs. cashew meal (blend)	½	c. oatmeal
1	Tbsp. salt	½	c. cornmeal
3	c. whole wheat flour	½	c. soy flour
¾	c. gluten flour	½	c. rye flour
½	c. barley flour		

Knead for 10 minutes. Let rise until double. Knead down. Let rise until double again. Form into loaves. Let rise until double.

Bake at 425 degrees for 10 minutes, then at 350 degrees for 40 minutes. Remove immediately from pans.

CHANGE OF FLAVOR IDEAS FOR BREAD

A. Use unsweetened fruit juice instead of water or use tomato juice instead of water.
B. Use vega-salt, onion salt, celery salt or garlic salt.
C. Add chopped dried fruit or nuts to batter.
D. Add chives (dried) or dried or fresh parsley or dried onions to the batter.

BREADS WITH FILLINGS

Pat out the dough for one loaf one inch thick and cover with filling. Roll up the dough and place in bread pan with the overlap at the bottom of your pan. This may be cut as rolls also.

FILLINGS

A. Finely ground nuts
B. Ground dried fruit
C. Finely ground orange or lemon peel
D. Combination of herbs such as sage and parsley or dill, sesame, celery or poppy seed; or sprinkle with garlic or onion powder and paprika, or use your imagination.
E. Homemade peanut butter mixed with ground raisins.
F. Sugarless jam

ONE LOAF BREAD

1	c. warm water	1	Tbsp. yeast
½	c. applesauce		

Mix and let stand 10 minutes, then add:

1	tsp. salt	2½	c. whole wheat flour

Knead well, adding flour if needed. Put in loaf pan and let rise to double in size.

Bake at 350 degrees for 45 to 50 minutes.

SUNNY SOYA BREAD

Put ½ cup lukewarm water in small bowl; sprinkle in:

1	Tbsp. dry yeast	¼	c. applesauce

In blender, mix together:

¼	c. applesauce	2	tsp. salt
1	c. cooked yellow squash	1	c. warm water

Mix until smooth. Pour into a large bowl.

Add:

2   c. whole wheat flour

Beat well, then add:

¼	c. wheat germ	½	c. soy flour
½	c. sunflower seeds		

Mix and add yeast, Stir in enough flour to make a soft bread dough, Knead until elastic. Put in Pam-sprayed bread pans. Let rise until double.

Bake for 35 to 40 minutes in a 375 degree oven.

WHEAT GERM MUFFINS

Mix together:

1¼	c. water	½	tsp. grated orange rind
½	c. applesauce		(optional)
2	tsp. yeast	1	c. wheat germ
½	tsp. salt		whole wheat pastry flour
½	tsp. vanilla		as needed
¾	c. raisins or dates	1/2	c. soy flour

Prepare muffin tins with Pam and fill to 2/3 full. Let rise 30 minutes. Preheat oven to 350 degrees.

Bake about 20 minutes. Watch carefully as they tend to burn easily.

Yield: 10 to 12 muffins.

ZUCCHINI WHEAT BREAD

In a large mixing bowl, combine:

¼	c. warm water	1	pkg. yeast

Let stand 5 minutes to soften. Add:

⅔	c. warm water	1	c. applesauce
3	Tbsp. oil or ½ avocado (mashed)		

Stir together:

1½	c. wl. wheat flour	1	tsp. salt
1½	c. unbleached white flour	1	tsp. grated orange rind
¼	c. wheat germ	2	tsp. ground cardamon

With a spoon, stir about half of this into the yeast mixture; add:

1½	c. coarsely shredded zucchini	¾	c. currants or raisins

Stir to blend. Gradually stir in ½ cup unbleached white flour.

Turn dough out onto a well floured board and knead 10 minutes, or until smooth and elastic, adding more flour as necessary to prevent sticking. Place dough in an oiled bowl, turning to oil top; cover and let rise in a warm place until doubled, about 1½ hours.

Punch down dough and divide in half. Shape and knead each half into a loaf and place in a loaf pan. Cover and let rise in a warm place about 45 minutes until the dough doubles.

Bake at 350 degrees for 40 to 45 minutes, or until tops are dark brown. Turn out onto racks to cool.

Makes 2 loaves.

To make Herb Zucchini Wheat Bread: Follow directions above, but OMIT orange rind, cardamon, and currants. Add ½ teaspoon dry basil, ¼ teaspoon thyme leaves, ¼ teaspoon oregano leaves to flour.

FOREIGN-STYLE FOODS

ARABIC POTATO SALAD

6	c. diced cooked potatoes	1	clove garlic, diced
1	c. diced onion	½	c. lemon juice
½	c. chopped parsley	1½	c. pineapple juice
1	tsp. dill seed		

Mix together.

BRAZILIAN RICE

2	cloves minced garlic	4	c. water
1	large onion, chopped	3	Tbs chicken- or beef-style
2	c. long grain brown rice		seasoning (McKay's)

Cook until rice is done, then add:

3	c. chopped tomatoes	½	c. chopped peanuts or cashews

Serve immediately

CEYLONESE RICE

Mix together in a large skillet:

2	c. cooked brown rice	1	bunch scallions cut in 1 inch lengths
1½	c. thin carrot strips		
1	c. chopped onion	½	c. raisins

Cook, stirring frequently, until vegetables just begin to brown, about 5 minutes. Add:

2	c. water	2	tsp. salt
1	pkg. (10 oz.) fzn. peas		

Bring to boiling, separating peas with a fork. Reduce heat; cover and simmer for 5 minutes.

Add 1 cup cashew nuts or pecan halves. Toss lightly.

Makes 8 to 10 servings.

CUBAN BLACK BEANS

Soak 1 cup black beans in water overnight. Drain. Add 2 cups cold water. Bring to boil, reduce heat. Then add:

1	small chopped onion	1	clove garlic, minced
½	chopped green pepper	1	tsp. salt

Simmer until done.

Serves 5 to 6.

GERMAN SOUP

Combine:

4	Tbsp. Beef-style McKay's seasoning	½	c. parsley
3	c. water	2	bay leaves, crushed
2	cans tomatoes or	¼	tsp. thyme
4	c. fresh tomatoes	4	c. diced potatoes
¼	c. lemon juice	4	c. diced onions
1	c. sauerkraut	1	c. shredded carrots
2	cloves garlic, minced	2	tsp. celery seed

Simmer for 1 hour.

INDIAN VEGETABLES

In a large skillet, cook until fork tender:

1½	c. water	1	tsp. salt
1	c. tomato puree	1	tsp. cumin
3	sliced potatoes	1	tsp. turmeric (more or less to taste)
2	thinly sliced onions		

Add:

3	c. tomatoes, chopped	2	c. cooked pinto beans
1	can cut green beans		

Heat and serve over rice.

ITALIAN GREENS SAUCE
(For Pasta or Grain)

Cook:

2	large onions, chopped	¼	c. water
4	cloves garlic, minced		

Add:

3	c. cashew cream	3	pkgs. frozen Swiss chard, thawed and drained and chopped

Heat and serve.

ITALIAN POLENTA

In a kettle, mix together:

1	c. crs. grd. cornmeal	1	Tbsp. chicken-style seasoning (McKay's)
3	c. water or tomato juice		

Cook until thick and done. Put into a loaf pan while hot. Cool, slice, cover with ground nuts and brown until crisp in broiler.

ITALIAN VEGETABLE SAUCE

Cook for 20 minutes:

1	lg. eggplant, cubed or	3	onions, finely chopped
3	c. zucchini, cubed	1	c. water

Add:

3	cloves garlic	½	c. chopped parsley
2	lbs. tomatoes, chopped	2	c. chopped olives
1	tsp. basil		salt, as needed

Simmer until thick. Serve on pasta.

ITALIANO VEGETABLE SOUP

Mix together:

2	quarts hot water	1	can (16 oz.) tomatoes
1	c. finely chopped onion	½	c. brown rice
1	c. finely sliced celery	2	Tbsp. chicken-style seasoning (McKay's)
1	c. finely sliced carrots		
1	c. chopped cabbage	½	tsp. thyme
1	c. cubed potatoes	¼	tsp. oregano
1	bay leaf, crumbled		

Simmer for 45 to 60 minutes.

MEXICAN AVOCADO DRESSING

Blend:

½	c. raw cashews	½	medium onion
1	c. water		

When smooth, add:

2	avocados	2	Tbsp. lemon juice

Blend until creamy.

MEXICAN AVOCADO HUEVOS RANCHEROS

Pour 2 tablespoons water into a frying pan over medium heat; add 1 medium-sized onion, chopped; cook until limp. Then stir in:

1	lg. can (15 oz.) tomato sauce	1	tsp ground cumin
1	clove garlic, minced	1	tsp. oregano leaves
3	Tbsp. seeded and chopped canned green chiles	1	bay leaf

Simmer, uncovered, 10 minutes or longer, until slightly thickened. Season to taste with salt. Cool, cover, and chill as long as 24 hours, if made ahead. Remove bay leaf and reheat, uncovered, to simmering before serving.

Peel, pit, and halve 2 avocados; coat cut sides with 2 tablespoons lemon juice and arrange, cut side up, in a 9 inch pie pan.

Spoon 1 to 2 tablespoons sauce over top. Broil, about 6 inches from heat.

Serve each avocado half on a bed of shredded lettuce. Pass remaining sauce to spoon over all.

Makes 4 servings.

MEXICAN ENCHILADAS

Thaw frozen tortillas and dip, one at a time, in tomato juice. Place each tortilla on a large plate and spread with refried beans. Place a heaping tablespoon of enchilada sauce across the center of the tortilla. Roll up the filled tortillas and place loosely in a baking dish. Cover all with more enchilada sauce.

Bake at 300 degrees for 30 minutes, until hot.

ENCHILADA SAUCE

4	c. chopped onions	½	Tbsp. chicken-style seasoning (McKay's)
1	c. chopped mushrooms		
1	c. chopped olives	1	tsp. oregano
1	c. tomato juice	2	(6 oz.) cans tomato paste
½	tsp. garlic salt	2	(8 oz.) cans tomato sauce

Simmer 2 hours.

MEXICAN GUACAMOLE

2	lg. tomatoes, chopped fine	½	tsp. garlic salt
		1	tsp. salt
1	medium sized onion chopped fine	3	large avocados, finely cubed or mashed

Mix together.

MEXICAN BEANS

Soak 1 cup pinto or red beans overnight. Drain. Add and cook until well done:

1	lg. chopped onion	2½	c. water
½	tsp. garlic salt	½	tsp. salt

Mash the beans slightly and add:

¼	tsp. oregano	¼	tsp. turmeric
¼	tsp. cumin		

Use as you would refried beans.

MEXICAN BEANS WITH CHILES

3	c. cooked and mashed red beans	1	(4 oz.) can drained and diced green chilies
1	onion, minced salt, as needed	¾	tsp. oregano

Bake until hot and bubbly.

MEXICAN CORN

1	can corn	2	c. tomatoes
1	c. olives (sliced)	1	tsp. oregano

Combine; heat and serve.

MEXICAN RICE

1	c. brown rice	1	medium onion, chopped
1¼	c. water	¼	tsp. garlic salt
1	c. tomato sauce	1	tsp. cumin
½	tsp. oregano		

Combine and cook until done; add salt, as desired.
Just before serving, add 1 can of corn.

MEXICAN SALAD DRESSING

2	c. tomato juice	1	Tbsp. food yeast
⅓	c. lemon juice		(Brewers yeast)
¼	c. dried onion	½	c. olives
¼	c. dried parsley		
	vegetable seasoning salt, if needed		

Blend well.

MEXICAN-STYLE VEGETABLE RICE

Heat 3 tablespoons water in a frying pan over medium heat. Add:

1	large onion, chopped	1½	c. long grain brown rice
2	cloves garlic, minced		

Cook, stirring, until onion is limp and rice is opaque. Stir in:

½	tsp. salt	3	c. water
3	tsp. chicken-style seasoning (McKay's)		

Bring to boiling, cover and simmer 20 minutes, or until liquid is absorbed. To the rice, add:

1	(10 oz.) fzn. peas and carrots, thawed	1½	c. peeled, seeded, and chopped tomatoes

Stir just until blended. Cook over low heat, stirring just until vegetables are heated through, about 3 minutes.

MEXICAN TOSTADAS

Warm tortillas in a Teflon pan and keep warm in the oven. Cover with a towel. Place the tortilla on a plate and top with chili beans or pinto beans and a tossed green salad.

Use Mexican Salad Dressing or Avocado Dressing or Guacamole.

ORIENTAL CHINESE RICE

Cook:

1	c. chopped onion	1	c. water
1	c. chopped celery	1	Tbsp. chicken-style
2	c. sliced mushrooms		seasoning (McKay's)

(Add chicken-style seasoning to water; cook vegetables in this seasoned water.)

Add:

1	can water chestnuts, sliced	3	Tbsp. soy sauce
		3	c. cooked brown rice

Simmer 10 minutes.

ORIENTAL DRESSING FOR VEGETABLES

½	c. sesame seed paste	10	dates
3	Tbsp. lemon juice	½	c. hot water
2	Tbsp. soy sauce		

Blend.

ORIENTAL SOYBEANS

Soak, cook and drain 1 cup soybeans. Set aside.

Cook until tender, but crisp:

1	lg. onion, chopped	1	clove garlic, finely grated
2	large carrots, sliced	1	c. water

Add:

1	can pineapple chunks	1	Tbsp. chicken-style
2	tomatoes, chopped		seasoning (McKay's)

1	Tbsp. soy sauce	2	c. pineapple juice
2	Tbsp. cornstarch		

Add the soybeans and cook for about 2 minutes. Serve over brown rice.

ORIENTAL SWEET 'N' SAUCY RICE

Combine:

2	c. cooked brown rice	1	Tbsp. lemon juice
½	c. raisins	½	c. chopped almonds
½	c. pineapple juice		

Can be served hot or cold.

ORIENTAL SWEET-SOUR SAUCE

Heat:

1	qt. pineapple juice	1	tsp. onion salt
8	oz. orange juice	2	Tbsp. soy sauce
½	c. lemon juice		

Thicken slightly with cornstarch.

ORIENTAL VEGETABLES

To prepare, use a large skillet or several small pans. Cook vegetables briefly in seasoned water [2 tablespoons chicken-style (McKay's) seasoning in 1 quart of water].

You can use any combination of these vegetables your family likes:

thin zucchini slices
thin diagonally cut celery
Chinese pea pods
green pepper strips
bamboo shoots
green onions, cut
lengthwise or onion rings

quartered tomatoes
whole green beans
bean sprouts
water chestnuts
fresh or canned
mushrooms

Serve the vegetables on brown rice and top generously with the Sweet-Sour Sauce and whole or sliced almonds.

PARISIAN GREEN LIMAS

In separate pans, cook:

| 1 | lg. pkg. green limas | 1 | pkg. broccoli spears |

Place hot broccoli in casserole; pour on hot limas and 1 large can mushroom slices.

Blend:

| 1 | c. raw cashews | 1 | Tbsp. chicken-style |
| 2 | c. hot water | | seasoning (McKay's) |

Pour over vegetables. Heat to bubbling in a 350 degree oven. Serve.

PORTUGUESE RED BEAN SOUP

Cook about 10 to 15 minutes:

| 1 | quart water | 1 | large potato, unpeeled, |
| 1 | c. whl. wheat macaroni | | chopped |

Add and cook 5 minutes:

| 1 | small head cabbage, coarsely chopped | 1 | quart water |

Add and heat:

1	c. tomato sauce	1	tsp. paprika
1	Tbsp. onion powder	4	c. cooked red beans
1	tsp. garlic powder		

PORTUGUESE ZUCCHINI

Cook:

1	finely chopped onion	2	c. water
1	c. soaked red beans	1	tsp. Italian-herb
1	6 oz. can tomato paste		seasoning

When the beans are done, add salt if needed and 3 or 4 medium zucchini, sliced in ⅛ inch pieces. Simmer for about 10 minutes, until crisp-tender.

Serve.

PUERTO RICAN BEANS AND RICE

1	lg. onion, diced	½	tsp. garlic salt
1	8 oz. can tomato sauce	1	c. water
1	tsp. oregano	2	c. tomato juice

Cook until onions are done.

Add:

4	c. cooked navy or pinto beans	4	c. cooked brown rice

PUNJAB PEA SOUP

Bring to a boil and simmer for 1 hour:

1	med. onion, fine chopped	1	c. dried split peas
1	tsp. turmeric	1	clove garlic, minced
½	tsp. cumin	1	bay leaf, crumbled
5	c. water	2	Tbsp. chicken-style
2	med. carrots, sliced		seasoning (McKay's)
1	Tbsp. celery seed	⅛	tsp. thyme
⅛	tsp. rosemary		

Blend and serve.

SPANISH GAZPACHO (A Cold Soup)

1	c. chopped tomato	½	tsp. celery seed
½	c. chopped cucumbers	2	Tbsp lemon juice
½	c. finely chopped green onion	¼	tsp. garlic powder
		1	thinly sliced zucchini
¼	c. snipped parsley	3	c. tomato juice
1	Tbsp. soy sauce		

Combine and chill for at least 4 hours.

SUKIYAKI

Cook for 5 minutes:

1	c. water	1	c. thinly sliced onions

Add and cook for 5 minutes more:

1	pkg. frozen French-style green beans	1	pkg. broccoli spears, cut lengthwise if large

Add and cook for 2 minutes:

1	lg can sliced mushrooms	2	c. tofu cubes
1	can No. 2½ bean sprouts		

Thicken slightly and serve with soy sauce.

FRUITS

ALMOST ALMOND ROCA

1	c. walnuts, ground	½	c. orange juice
1	c. raw almonds, ground	3	Tbsp. Minute Tapioca
1	c. coconut, ground	1	tsp. vanilla
1	c. dates, ground		ground nuts for rolling
3	Tbsp. carob powder		

Grind nuts and dates through coarse blade of food grinder. Place nuts, dates, coconut and carob powder in mixing bowl. Combine in small saucepan, the orange juice and tapioca. Cook and stir over medium heat until tapioca is clear, about 6 to 8 minutes. Add vanilla.

Combine all ingredients and mix thoroughly. (Fingers work best!) Roll small portions between palms of hands into logs, about 1½ inches in length. Roll logs in ground nuts. Chill until firm.

Yield: 2 to 3 dozen pieces.

Store in refrigerator.

APPLE DATE SQUARES

Mix together:

2½	c. oats	½	c. coconut
1	c. whl. wheat flour	½	c. chopped nuts

Spread ¾ of this crumb mixture in a 9 x 12 inch pan.

Filling:

4	c. shredded apples	3	c. orange juice
1	c. chopped dates	1	tsp. vanilla

Pour the filling over the crumb mixture in the pan. Top with the rest of the crumb mixture and bake at 350 degrees for 30 minutes.

ARMENIAN CHRISTMAS PORRIDGE

Combine and cook for 45 minutes:

1	c. pearl barley	1	quart water

Add and cook 30 minutes more, uncovered:

2	c. chopped dried apricots	1	tsp. salt
1½	c. raisins	½	tsp. ground coriander
1	quart water		

Turn off heat, cover, but leave on burner 1 hour.

Serve warm with nut milk. (This porridge can be cooled and reheated.)

NUT MILK

½	c. raw nuts (cashews, almonds)	½	c. dates
			dash of salt
1 1/2	c. hot water	1	tsp. vanilla

Thoroughly blend together.

BAKED OATMEAL

Combine:

2½	c. rolled oats	1	c. raisins or dates
4	large apples, sliced	1	tsp salt
1	c. chopped nuts	1	tsp. cinnamon or sub.

Add 1 teaspoon vanilla to 3 cups apple juice and pour over oat mixture. Mix thoroughly. Pour into Pam-sprayed pan.

Bake for 1 hour at 350 degrees.

Serve with nut milk and nuts on top.

Can be made the night before and put on time-bake. The aroma is pleasant to awaken to!

BANANA CREAM PUDDING OR PIE

Blend:

1	c. raw cashews	1½	tsp. vanilla
2	c. hot water	½	tsp. salt
24	dates	4	Tbsp. cornstarch

Add 1 cup hot water; cook until thickened. Cool and add 4 sliced bananas.

BANANA NUT COOKIES

Blend:

½	c. dates	¾	c. hot water
½	c. raw cashews		

Add and mix well:

6	mashed bananas	3	c. raw rolled oats
1½	c. chopped nuts	2	tsp. vanilla
1½	c. whl. wheat flour	1	tsp. salt

Drop by spoonfuls on a cookie sheet.

Bake at 325 degrees until light brown.

BERRY TOPPINGS

Heat and thicken slightly, 16 ounces apple juice concentrate. Add 1 quart berries and serve on waffles, pancakes, toast or cereals.

BREAD OR RICE PUDDING

Blend:

1	c. raw cashews	2	tsp. vanilla
2	c. dates	2	tsp. cinnamon
3	c. hot water		

Pour over:

4	c. cooked brown rice or 6 c. whl. wheat bread cubes mixed with 1½ c. raisins	1	c. chopped walnuts

Bake at 350 degrees for 25 minutes.

CAROB CANDY

Melt slowly on *low* heat:

4	c. old-fash. p.nut butter	4	c. date-sweetened carob chips

Pour this over 4 cups raisins and 2 large cans crisp oriental noodles.

Cool in refrigerator. This makes a large quantity, but freezes well.

CAROB FRUIT BARS

Dissolve 1 tablespoon dry yeast in ¼ cup hot water.
Add:

1½	c. cut up prunes	1	c. whl. wheat flour
1	c. raisins	3	Tbsp. carob powder
1	c. dates, chopped	1	c. chopped nuts

Spread 1 inch thick in baking pan and let rise 30 minutes. Bake at 325 degrees for 40 minutes.

CAROB PUDDING

Cook 5 minutes:

1   c. water   ¼ to ⅓ c. carob powder

Cool slightly.

Blend until smooth:

1   c. hot water   1   c. raw cashews

Add and continue to blend:

1   c. hot water   2   c. dates

Combine all ingredients and add:

2   Tbls. vanilla   ¼   c. cornstarch

Bring all to a slow boil to thicken, stirring constantly.

Cool in a covered dish.

Serve topped with sliced bananas or carob syrup.

CAROB SYRUP

Cook 5 minutes:

1   c. water   ½   c. carob powder

Cool slightly.

Blend:

2   c. hot water   2   c. dates

Combine ingredients.

Use as you would chocolate syrup on banana slices or carob pudding.

CAROB SUPER FUDGE

½   c. carob powder   ½   c. water

Mix carob powder in water. Boil, stirring, for 5 minutes, until a smooth paste is formed.

Add and Mix well:

1   c. peanut butter   1   c. walnuts, chopped
½   c. coconut, shredded,   1   tsp. vanilla
    unsweetened
1   c. date butter (1 c.
    chopped dates cooked in
    ½ c. water until very soft)

Press into square pan. Refrigerate.

Cut into squares to serve. Decorate with walnut half on top.

Yield: 2 dozen pieces.

CASHEW CREAM OR MILK

Blend until smooth:

1   c. raw cashews   ½   tsp. vanilla
1   c. hot water   dash of salt
8   dates

Cool before serving.

For milk, use 3 to 4 cups water.

COMPANY OATMEAL

2   c. rolled oats   ⅛   tsp. coriander plus
1   lg., unpeeled apple,   1/16 tsp. cardamon
     cored and sliced   1   tsp. vanilla plus
¼   c. unsweetened coconut ⅛   tsp. coconut extract
¼   c. chopped nuts   1   tsp. salt
¾   c. raisins   4   c. water

Stir seasonings into water. Combine all ingredients.

Bake for 1 hour at 350 degrees.

COOL AND CREAMY OATMEAL

Combine and refrigerate overnight:

2	c. raw oatmeal	1	c. chopped nuts or seeds
2	c. orange juice	¼	tsp. salt

Just before serving, add 4 cups of any berries or fresh, frozen or canned fruit.

DANISH APPLE CAKE

Using a 9 x 12 inch baking dish, spread 1½ cups dried bread crumbs in the dish. Top with 2 cups applesauce. Repeat layers as above, ending with ½ cup crumbs.

Bake 30 minutes at 350 degrees.

Serve with Cashew Cream.

DATE APPLE COOKIES

Blend:

1½	c. dates	¾	c. raw cashews
1½	c. hot water		

Add:

2	c. finely chopped apple	1	tsp. vanilla
½	c. chopped walnuts	1	c. raisins
½	tsp. salt	3	c. rolled oats

Form cookies on baking sheet.

Bake at 350 degrees for 25 minutes.

DATE-COCONUT CRUST

Cover 1 cup dates with enough water to blend into a very thick paste. May need to add a few more dates.

Add:

½	c. coconut unsweetened	1	tsp. lemon or orange rind grated

Blend. Spoon and spread into pie pan. Don't make it too thick. Press chopped walnuts (or other nuts) all over and freeze.

FROZEN DESSERT

Blend:

2	c. apple or pineapple juice

Add *frozen* fruit until very thick.

Fruit can be any unsweetened berries and/or bananas.

To freeze bananas just peel ripe ones and put in plastic bags. Freeze at once.

FRUIT CAKE - NUMBER 1

In large bowl, soften 3 tablespoons dry yeast in ½ cup warm apple juice. In saucepan, combine:

¾	c. applesauce	1	c. apple juice

Place over low heat to remove chill. Add to yeast mixture.

Stir in:

½	c. nut cream*	1½	c. rye flour
1½	c. whl. wheat flour	1	tsp. salt

Mix together:

1	c. prunes, pitted and cut	½	tsp. lemon rind
1	c. dried apricots, cut	½	c. sesame seeds
1	c. dates, cut	½	c. nuts or sunflower seeds
½	tsp. ground anise seed		

Mix thoroughly with batter. Place in Pam-sprayed fruit cake or miniature bread pans to ¾ inch of top. Decorate tops with dried fruit flowers made by cutting dried apricots into several petal-shaped pieces surrounding a round center. Set in warm place.

When risen to top of pans, bake at 350 degrees for 1 hour. (Turn heat down to 325 degrees for the last 15 minutes if browned sufficiently.)

Yield: 4 small ¾ pound loaves.

*Nut cream is made by whizzing 1 cup water and ½ cup raw nuts in blender until smooth.

FRUIT CAKE - NUMBER 2

2	c. white raisins	½	c. orange juice
6	c. chopped dried fruit, (any combination of peaches, pears, etc.)	2	c. date butter*
		1	c. soy flour
		2	c. whl. wheat flour
2	c. chopped walnuts	1	c. cashew butter
2	c. crushed pineapple and juice		

Mix well and put in small loaf pans.

Bake for 2½ hours at 275 degrees.

*Date butter is made by blending 1½ cups dates and ½ cup hot water together.

FRUIT CANDY

1	c. (about ¼ lb.) dried figs	1	c. nuts (walnuts, pecans,
1	c. pitted dates		or almonds)
1	c. raisins	1	tsp. grated lemon or
1	c. dried apricots		orange rind
3	Tbsp. lemon juice		

Grind fruits and nuts together through fine blade of food grinder. Then add juice and rind. Line a pan with waxed paper. Pack fruit mixture well and smooth the top. Place a weight on top and let stand for a few hours. Then cut into squares.

Decorate tops with shredded coconut or walnut halves.

Optional additions: May add 1 cup peanut butter, ½ cup granola cereal to fruit after grinding.

Store in refrigerator or freezer.

FRUIT DELICACY

Grind coarsley:

1	c. dates	1	c. fresh coconut
1	c. dried apricots		unsweetened
1	c. raisins	1	c. walnuts

Form into small balls.

FRUITED OATS

Cook for 15 minutes:

4	c. water	2	c. lg. cooking rolled oats
1	tsp. salt		

Add 2 cups dried fruit; let mixture set until fruit has plumped.

You can also use 4 cups fresh or canned fruit.

FRUIT MEDLEY

Combine:

orange sections
seeded grapes
chopped apples

strawberries, whl. or half
banana slices
pineapple chunks w/juice

FRUIT WHIP

*Soak until puffy 3 cups dried fruit (any single kind or combination). Put 3 lemon slices in soaking water. Blend fruit and liquid until smooth and creamy.

Serve over brown rice or cereal or bread.

*Soak the dried fruit in juice instead of water.

GRANOLA

Combine and mix well:

10	c. raw oatmeal	1	tsp. salt
1	c. unsweetened coconut	2	c. apple- or pear-sauce
1	c. sunflower seeds		

Spread on cookie sheets and dry completely in a 200 degree oven.

It takes several hours.

GRANOLA DESSERTS

Number 1:

Combine equal amounts of any fruit sauce and granola and let stand several hours.

Number 2:

Combine and mix well:

2	c. peanut butter	2	c. hot water

Add:

1	c. sesame seeds	4	c. granola

HAYSTACKS

Blend until smooth:

3	c. dates	½	c. orange or pineapple
¼	c. hot water		juice

1½ c. raisins

Add:

4	c. unsweetened coconut	⅓	c. raw oatmeal
¾	c. whl. wheat flour	½	tsp. salt
1⅔	c. chopped walnuts		

Put tablespoonfuls on cookie sheets and bake at 300 degrees for 20 to 25 minutes. Watch closely as they burn easily.

JOHNNY APPLESEED RICE PUDDING

½	c. raw brown rice	⅛	tsp. salt
2	c. apple juice	½	c. raisins

Combine and bring to a boil. Cover and cook on low heat for 40 minutes.

1	c. chopped dates	1½	c. diced apples

Add and cook 10 minutes longer. Top with nuts and serve plain or with nut cream.

Yield: 6 servings.

LEMON PUDDING OR PIE

Blend:

1	c. warm pineapple juice	¼	c. water
1	c. warm orange juice	1	Tbsp. cornstarch
4	Tbsp. lemon juice	¼	tsp. salt
14	dates	¼	c. raw cashews

Cook until thickened. Cool.

LEMON SAUCE

3	tsp. lemon juice	3	Tbsp cornstarch
2	c. water	½	c. apple juice concentrate
1	tsp. grated lemon rind		

Cook until thick and clear.

Serve warm or cold.

NO-SUGAR APPLE PIE

1	12 oz. can fzn. apple juice concentrate	1	tsp. cinnamon or cardamon
3	Tbsp. cornstarch or arrowroot powder pinch of salt	5	lg. sweet eating apples, i.e., Golden Delicious, peeled and sliced

Combine juice, cornstrach, cinnamon, and salt. Heat until thickened. Add sliced apples and simmer until partially cooked.

Pour into unbaked pie shell and cover with top crust or crumb topping.

Bake at 350 degrees for 45 minutes.

ORANGE SAUCE

2	c. orange juice	½	tsp. celery salt
2	tsp. grated orange rind	2	Tbsp. cornstarch

Heat until thickened. Serve hot on squash, sweet potatoes, or cold on fruit salad.

PEAR DELIGHT

Blend and serve hot or cold:

1	c. almonds	1	c. dates
1	c. hot water	1	tsp. lemon peel
1	Tbsp. lemon juice	1	c. dried apricots
1	tsp. vanilla		

Serve over pear halves (fresh or canned) and top with chopped almonds.

PINEAPPLE TAPIOCA PUDDING

1½	c. pineapple juice	1	c. crushed pineapple
¼	c. Minute Tapioca		dash of salt

Mix all ingredients in saucepan; let stand for 5 minutes. Bring to a good boil over medium heat, stirring frequently. Cool 20 minutes and stir. Store in refrigerator.

Makes six ½ cup servings.

POLYNESIAN BARS

Mix and cook until consistency of jam:

2	c. chopped dates	1 20 oz. can crushed pineapple

Mix together:

1½	c. raw oatmeal	½	c. chopped nuts
½	c. millet flour	½	tsp. salt
1	c. coconut unsweetened	1	c. orange juice

Spread ¾ of the oat mixture in a 9 x 12 inch pan. Add date-pineapple mixture and top with the remaining oat mixture. Pat down.

Bake at 325 degrees for 30 minutes.

PUMPKIN PIE FILLING OR PUDDING

Blend:

½	c. raw cashews	1½	c. hot water
2	c. dates	2	Tbsp. cornstarch

Add and mix well:

1	large can pumpkin	1	tsp. vanilla
1	tsp. salt	2	tsp. cinnamon

Bake at 350 degrees for 30 minutes.

RAISIN-APPLE PIE FILLING

1	c. raisins	2	Tbsp. arrowroot powder,
4	c. diced apples		(or cornstarch)
½	c. dates	2	tsp. grated orange rind
	pinch of salt	½ to 1 c. fresh orange juice
1	baked 9 inch pie shell		

Wash raisins in colander; drain. Cook raisins, apples, dates, salt, orange juice until apples are tender. Moisten arrowroot with 1 tablespoon water; add to hot fruit and stir gently. Cook over low heat until glaze is clear. Add grated orange rind; stir gently.

Cool and pour into baked pie shell.

Serve warm or cold.

RASPBERRY DESSERT

Thaw and drain 2 quarts frozen raspberries. Heat and blend the juice and 1½ cups dates, or 12 ounces frozen apple juice concentrate.

Add the berries to the juice and pour over 6 cups fresh whole wheat bread, cubed.

This can be served hot or cold.

For a strawberry or blueberry dessert, heat 12 ounces apple juice concentrate (for blueberry use grape juice) and pour over berries and bread cubes.

RAW APPLESAUCE

½   c. pineapple juice   2   Golden Delicious apples

Put juice in blender. Wash apples and remove stem and blossom-end. Cut in pieces. Add to juice in blender; blend until smooth.

Makes delicious sauce served plain, over French toast, or in sherbet glasses with crushed nuts on top.

Four pitted dates may be added while blending, if desired.

RICE PUDDING

Mix in a bowl:

½   c. peanut butter   2   c. apple juice

Add:

2   c. raisins or chopped   4   c. cooked brown rice
     dates

Put in a baking dish and bake in the oven for 30 minutes at 375 degrees.

SCALLOPED APPLES

Combine:

4   c. fresh whl. wheat bread   6   c. chopped raw apples
     crumbs

Blend and add:

1   c. dates, packed   ½   c. raw cashews
1½   c. hot water

Bake for 45 minutes at 325 degrees.
Serve with Fruit Sauce.

FRUIT SAUCE

Combine and blend:

12	oz. apple juice conc.	2	Tbsp. lemon juice
½	c. raw cashews		grated lemon peel
1½	c. hot water	2	Tbsp. cornstarch

Heat mixture until thick.

SCANDINAVIAN FRUIT SOUP

Combine and heat:

2½	c. dried fruits, chopped	1	quart apple juice
½	tsp. anise	2	c. orange juice
½	lemon, sliced thin	1	can pineapple chunks
1	c. raisins		with juice

Thicken with tapioca or cornstarch.

SESAME BARS - NUMBER 1

Blend:

2	c. dates	1½	c. hot water
1	c. raw cashews		

Add:

1	c. unsweetened coconut	2	c. sesame seeds
1	c. sunflower seeds		

Bake at 300 degrees for 30 minutes.

SESAME BARS - NUMBER 2

Mix:

1½	c. date butter	½	c. sunflower seeds
½	c. cashew meal	1	c. sesame seeds
½	c. coconut		

Bake at 300 degrees for 20 to 30 minutes.

SHERBET

Blend:

1	c. orange juice conc.	6	ripe bananas
1	c. water		

Add, folding in carefully, 1 can crushed pineapple.

Freeze in ice cube trays.

STEAMED PUDDING

Soak overnight in enough apple juice just to cover:

1	c. raisins	1	c. ea. chopped dried apricots, prunes, and apples

Blend:

1	c. hot water	½	c. raw cashews
10	dates		

Combine:

	dried fruit with juice	2	c. whl. wheat flour
½	tsp. salt	2	Tbsp. grated lemon rind
2	c. fresh whole wheat bread crumbs		nut milk

Put all in a Pam-sprayed tube pan and steam 2 hours in a covered steamer, cool, unmold, slice and serve topped with warm or cold apple sauce.

TAPIOCA DESSERTS

Thicken 1 quart of any fruit juice with tapioca or tapioca flour.
Cool and add 1 quart of fruit.

TROPICAL FRUIT SALAD

Combine:

chunks of fresh pineapple	bananas, diag. sliced
papayas, cubed	fresh lime wedges

YUMMY COOKIE BARS

Blend:

2	c. dates	2	c. warm apple juice conc.

Add and mix well:

2	tsp. vanilla	1	c. peanut butter

Add and mix:

1	c. chopped nuts	1	c. coconut (unsweetened)
1	c. raisins	3	c. whl. wheat flour
2	c. rolled oats	¾	c. soy flour

Spread about one inch deep in baking pans and bake at 300 degrees for 30 to 45 minutes.

Cut in bars while still warm.

Write your extra recipes here:

GRAVIES

BROWN GRAVY

6 to	8 Tbsp. whl. wheat flour, depending on thickness desired	¼	tsp. onion salt
		⅛	tsp. garlic salt
		⅛	tsp. celery salt
2	c. cold water	1	tsp. minced dehydrated onion
½	tsp. salt		
2	tsp. soy sauce		

Combine flour and water and stir until well blended. Cook over low heat until thick. Add remaining ingredients and cook slowly for 5 to 10 minutes, stirring occasionally.

CASHEW GRAVY

Blend until smooth:

2	c. hot water	½	tsp. onion powder
¾	c. raw cashews	½	tsp. garlic powder
1	Tbsp. Brewer's yeast		

Add chicken- or beef-style seasoning (McKay's) to taste. Heat just to boiling.

ONION GRAVY

Dice 2 large onions. Mix water and soy sauce to make 4 cups, the flavor you want. Simmer 30 minutes. Thicken with cornstarch. Add sliced mushrooms and/or sliced olives, if desired.

QUICK TOMATO GRAVY

¼	tsp. Italian herb s'soning	½	tsp. onion powder or
¼	tsp. cumin	1	Tbsp. dried onion
3	c. tomato juice	2	Tbsp. cornstarch

Cook until thick.

JAMS AND FRUIT RELISHES

APPLE BUTTER

Blend:

12 oz. warm apple juice	**1 tsp.** cinnamon or cardamon

Add dried apples until thick.

APRICOT JAM

Blend:

2 c. warm pineapple juice	**1 c.** dates

Add dried apricots until thick.

APRICOT - PINEAPPLE BUTTER

Blend:

4 lbs. fresh apricots	**2 c.** dates

(Should make 7 cups puree.) Add:

1 can crushed pineapple

Simmer, stirring constantly, until thickened.

BERRY JAM

Blend:

2 c. fresh or thawed berries

Add dried apples while blender is going, until mixture is thick.

COOKED CRANBERRY SAUCE

Cook:

1 pkg. fresh raw cranberries	**6 oz.** orange juice conc.
	12 oz. apple juice conc.

Sieve and thicken with tapioca flour or cornstarch.

Cool before serving.

CRANBERRY RELISH

Grind:

1	pkg. fresh raw cran-berries	4	lg. cored apples
		2	unpeeled oranges

Add:

12   oz. apple juice conc.

Let stand 24 hours before serving.

DATE JAM

1	c. raisins	1	c. water
1	c. dates		

Blend.

PEACH OR PEAR JAM

Blend 12 ounces warm apple juice adding dried peaches or pears until thick.

PRUNE JAM

Blend 12 ounces warm orange juice adding dried prunes until thick.

RAISIN JAM

Blend:

2	c. warm grape juice	½	c. almonds
2	c. raisins	1	tsp. cardamon or cinnamon

RASPBERRY JAM

1	c. grape, apple, or pineapple juice	1½	Tbsp. cornstarch
8	chopped dates	1¼	to 1½ c. boysenberries rasp- or blueberries

Puree first 3 ingredients and bring to a boil; cook gently for 5 to 8 minutes. Then add berries. If the juice isn't the color of the berries, puree ¼ cup with the juice.

SYRUP

Blend:

2	**c. fruit juice**	**10**	**dates**
1	**Tbsp. cornstarch**		

Cook to thicken and serve hot or cold on french toast, waffles, or toasted whole grain bread.

Write an extra recipe here:

MAIN DISHES

HOW TO COOK DRY BEANS

Method 1:

Sort beans carefully. Wash with cold water in colander. Add beans to boiling water in large kettle. Bring to full boil. Turn off heat. Let stand for an hour or more. Bring to boiling and let boil until tender (about an hour). Add salt and simmer until well done.

Note: There is some evidence that beans cooked by this method cause less flatulence (gas).

Method 2:

Soak beans overnight. Drain. Add drained beans to rapidly boiling water. Heat to boiling point. Boil gently until tender; add salt. Simmer until well done.

Note: Some have found that 1 teaspoon unflavored meat tenderizer, 1 part dry papaya in the tenderizer, contains the enzymes which change the hulls of the beans so they do not cause gas in the intestines. Hot water inactivates the enzymes, so should not be used for soaking beans.

To one cup of beans, add 3 to 4 cups water. For lentils, use 3 cups only. Lentils and split peas may be cooked in one-half hour, and should not be soaked. Black, pinto, great northern, kidney and navy eans cook in about 3 to 5 hours, or 45 minutes in a pressure cooker. Soy beans and garbanzos will take five to eight hours to be palatable and tender, or one hour and twenty minutes in a pressure cooker. To be digested well, beans need to be cooked until hulls have burst and beans are very tender. Overnight cooking in a crock pot works well.

Note: Add salt during very last part of the cooking time. Some feel this helps to reduce the distress factor.

Combinations of legumes and grains make a perfect protein such as peanut butter (a legume on whole grain bread (3 grain).

BAKED BEANS

Combine:

4	c. cooked navy beans	1	c. tomato paste
1	c. chopped onion		

Blend and add:

1	c. pitted dates	¾	c. hot water

Bake 2 hours at 300 degrees.

BAKED NUT RICE

2	c. cooked brown rice	½	c. water
½	c. creamy peanut butter	2	Tbsp. dried onion

Bake at 375 degrees until hot, about 20 to 30 minutes.

You can add 1 cup dried fruit or 2 cups fresh fruit instead of the onion for a fruit meal.

BEANS AND RICE

Equal amounts of each ingredient:

cooked brown rice
cooked red beans

fzn., fresh or canned corn
tomato sauce

Season this dish with cumin and garlic powder for a Mexican flavor.

CARROT - RICE

Combine:

2	c. grated raw carrots	1	c. whl. wheat crumbs
1	c. cooked brown rice or millet or barley	1	c. tomato juice
		1	c. chopped olives
½	c. grated raw onion	1	tsp. sage
1	chopped nuts	1	tsp. salt

Bake for 1 hour at 325 degrees.

CASHEW VEGETABLE DISH

Combine and saute in ⅓ cup water:

½	c. diced onions	½	c. chopped fresh
½	c. diced celery		mushrooms optional

Add:

2	c. garbanzos or limas, cooked and lightly mashed	1	tsp. sweet basil
		1	Tbsp. chicken-style seasoning (McKay's)
¼	c. parsley, chopped	1	c. chopped raw cashews

Heat and serve.

CRACKED WHEAT AND ALMOND PILAF

2	c. Ala bulgar wheat or cr'ked wheat (see below)	2	c. boiling water
		1	c. sliced almonds (raw)
1	c. chopped celery	1½	tsp. salt
8	grn. onions, sliced fine	¼	tsp. marjoram
2	c. broth or bouillon, (vegetable)	½	tsp. oregano

Brown celery and onions lightly in Pam-sprayed pan; add Ala and brown. Place in a 2 quart casserole and pour bouillon and boiling water over top. Blend in almonds, salt, marjoram and oregano.

Cover and bake in a 325 degree oven for 1½ hours.

Note: If you have a blender or a flour mill, you can combine three of four whole grains (such as wheat, rye, brown rice, and barley) and crack them yourself for this recipe. Combining several whole grains together enhances the protein quality and provides more abundant supplies of all nutrients.

Note: Ala can be found in your local supermarket under the trade name of Fisher's Ala. It should be located with the brown rice and other grain items.

GARDEN RICE

Combine and cook only until the spinach wilts:

1	lb. sliced fresh spinach	½	c. ea. of finely diced grn. onions and celery
1	c. water chestnuts, sliced		
¼	c. water		

Stir in:

2	c. cooked brown rice	1	tsp. chicken-style seasoning (McKay's)
¼	tsp. rosemary		

Heat and serve.

GLUTEN

Mix and let stand (covered) for 1 hour:

2	c. Do-Pep	1	c. whl. wheat flour
3	c. warm water		

Broth: Mix in a large baking pan with a cover:

1½	c. old-fash. peanut butter	⅓	c. soy sauce
6	c. warm water		

Divide the gluten into small pieces and put into the broth. Bake at 300 degrees for one hour.

HERB RICE

1	c. brown rice	½	c. chopped onion
2	c. tomato juice	¼	c. chopped parsley
½	tsp. celery salt	½	tsp. grated lemon peel
¼	tsp. oregano, rosemary and thyme		

Combine and cook according to rice directions.

LENTILS AND RICE

Combine equal amounts:

cooked brown rice	½	amount chopped onions,
cooked lentils		cooked

This will need little or no salt.

LENTIL ROAST

Soak 4 cups cubed bread in 1 cup nut milk.

Add:

2	c. cooked lentils	½	tsp. sage
¾	c. chopped nuts	½	chopped onion
1	tsp. salt		

Bake 1 hour at 325 degrees.

MACARONI AND CASHEW NUT "CHEESE" SAUCE

Cook:

1	c. macaroni, enriched, (or whl. wheat)	1	qt. boiling water
		½	tsp. salt

Crumbs:

¼	c. whl. wheat crumbs	1	Tbs. Brewer's flake yeast

Sauce:

½	c. cashew nuts (raw)	1	tsp. salt
2	oz. jar pimentos	¼	tsp. onion powder
¼	c. lemon juice		speck of garlic powder
3	Tbs. Brewer's flake yeast	1½	c. water

Add macaroni to boiling, salted water. Cook, uncovered, 15 minutes. Mix lightly. Do not drain cooking water.

While macaroni is cooking, combine "cheese" sauce ingredients in blender until smooth. Add to macaroni. Salt to taste.

Put in casserole; cover.

Bake at 350 degrees for 30 minutes. Sprinkle with crumbs and bake, uncovered, for 15 minutes.

You can substitute almonds or peanuts for cashew nuts, if desired.

MILLET ENTREE'

1	c. uncooked millet	½	c. sliced ripe olives
5	c. tomato juice	½	c. cashew pieces
1	medium onion, chopped	½	tsp. sage
½	tsp. salt	½	Tbsp. garlic powder or savory

Mix in the same entree' dish used for baking. Cover well with foil or well fitting lid so the moisture from the entree' won't escape.

Bake at 325 degrees for 2 hours, then bake at 250 degrees for 1 more hour.

Note: This entree' is delicious without gravy.

POTTAGE

Mix:

1	c. dry lentils	2	c. water
½	c. uncooked brown rice	1	c. mushrooms opt.

Blend and add:

1	c. olives	1	medium raw onion
¾	c. water		

Cook on low heat until done, about 45 minutes.

RICE STUFFING

3	c. cooked brown rice or millet or barley	1	c. slcd. mushrooms (opt.)
		½	c. nut butter
1	c. diced celery	1	Tbsp. soy sauce
1	c. diced onion		2 tsp. sage

Add whole grain bread crumbs for desired consistency. Bake as a loaf or stuff peppers, eggplant, or acorn squash.

SESAME SEED PILAF

Cook until rice is done:

1	lg. onion, chopped	2	c. water
1	clove garlic, minced	1	Tbsp. chicken-style seasoning (McKay's)
1	c. brown rice		

Add 1 package (10 ounces) thawed frozen peas and ½ cup toasted sesame seeds. Mix and top with ¼ cup sesame seeds.

SOYBEAN SOUFFLE

Soak:

1½	c. soybeans overnight and drain

Blend thoroughly:

	soybeans	2½	c. warm water
1	onion		

Add:

2	tsp. salt	1	tsp. garlic powder

1½ c. rolled wheat, oats or barley

Bake 2 hours at 300 degrees.

Serve with onion or tomato gravy.

SOYTEENA

1	c. dry soy beans, (2½ to 3 c. soaked and drained)	1	stalk celery
		¼	c. yeast flakes
2	c. water	½	medium onion
1	c. tomato juice	4	Tbsp. soy sauce
½	c. peanut butter		garlic salt to taste
2	tsp. salt	1	c. cornmeal

Combine all the ingredients, except the cornmeal, and put in blender until smooth. Remove from blender; add cornmeal. Pour into Pam-sprayed Number 2 cans and steam for 2 hours, or longer. (For slightly firmer texture, cover cans with foil and rubber bands.)

Steam in large kettle about ⅓ full of water when cans are set in it. *Keep water simmering with lid on.* When cooled, remove from cans.

Slice and serve on sandwiches.

TOMATO-LENTIL ON BREAD

Cook 30 minutes

2	c. uncooked lentils	½	tsp. cumin
1	c. chopped onions	¼	tsp. oregano
1	c. diced carrot	1	tsp. salt
4	c. tomato juice		

Pour over 3 cups fresh whole wheat bread crumbs.

Bake for 30 minutes at 300 degrees.

TOMATOES AND RICE

Mix in a bowl:

2	c. cooked brown rice	1	can cut green beans
1	c. chopped tomatoes	1	tsp. onion salt
1	c. chopped black olives		

Put in a baking dish and bake 30 minutes at 350 degrees.

VEGETABLE CASSEROLE

Combine:

1	eggplant, cubed	2	c. cooked kidney beans
½	tsp. garlic salt	2	c. cooked garbanzos
3	sm. zucchini, sliced	16	oz. tomato paste
3	med. onions, thinly sliced	¼	c. chopped parsley
		1	tsp. Ital. herb seasoning

Bake at 375 degrees for about 45 minutes, until vegetables are fork tender.

WALNUT - RICE STUFFING

Cook:

1	lg. chopped onion		salt as needed
1	c. brown rice	1	tsp. oregano
¼	c. minced parsley	½	tsp. thyme
1¾	c. water		scooped out portion of
2	Tbsp. lemon juice		tomatoes, zucchini, or eggplant

When the rice is done, add:

1   c. chopped walnuts

Use to stuff or fill tomatoes, zucchini, eggplant, or green peppers. (About 12 medium tomatoes, 2 large eggplants, 6 medium zucchini, or 8 to 10 medium green peppers.)

Bake, uncovered, at 350 degrees for 30 minutes.

WALNUT STUFFING BALLS

Combine:

4	c. bread crumbs	1	c. crs. chopped walnuts
½	c. finely chopped or grated onion	½	c. nut butter
1	tsp. celery seed	½	tsp. salt
½	c. chopped parsley	1	tsp. sage

Add just enough seasoned water [1½ teaspoons chicken-style seasoning (McKay's) to 1 cup hot water] to form 2 inch balls.

Bake on cookie sheets at 375 degrees for about 15 minutes, until crisp and brown.

ZUCCHINI - PEANUTS - BARLEY

Cook 1 cup barley in 3 cups vegetable broth or tomato juice.
Cook separately until crisp and tender:

4	med. zucchini, cut in julienne strips	1	c. water
		1½	tsp. chicken-style seasoning (McKay's)

Add 1½ cups coarsley ground peanuts.
Thicken slightly with cornstarch and serve over the barley.

ZUCCHINI - RICE CASSEROLE

Combine:

5	c. thinly sliced zucchini	½	tsp. sweet basil
1	c. finely chopped onion	½	tsp. oregano
2	chopped tomatoes	1	c. brown rice
½	tsp. garlic salt	1	c. water

Bake 40 minutes at 350 degrees.

Write an extra recipe here:

PATTIES

BEAN - OAT PATTIES

Mash 1½ cups cooked beans (any kind) in liquid in which they were cooked.

Add and mix well:

1	c. rolled oats	½	c. chopped onion
½	c. chopped nuts	½	tsp. sage
2	Tbsp. food yeast		salt to taste

Shape into patties and bake for 30 minutes at 350 degrees. Turn after 15 minutes.

Serve with tomato sauce or onion gravy.

BILLY BURGERS

2	c. cooked barley	¼	c. walnuts, ground
½	c. grated raw potato	½	tsp. thyme
1	chopped onion		salt

Add enough bread crumbs so patties hold together.

Bake at 325 degrees for 30 minutes.

GARBANZO - RICE PATTIES

Blend:

1½	c. soaked garbanzos and drained	1	small onion
		1	Tbsp. soy sauce
½	c. raw cashews	1¼	c. hot water

Add:

1½	c. cooked brown rice	1	Tbsp. Brewer's yeast
¼	tsp. garlic powder		

Form patties on cookie sheets and bake 30 minutes at 325 degrees.

LENTIL PATTIES

Combine and mix well:

2	c. well cooked lentils	2½ c. whole wheat bread

1	c. chopped onion		crumbs or cooked brown rice
½	c. ground walnuts	½	tsp. sage
1	tsp. salt	2	Tbsp. soy sauce

Add enough nut milk to form patties. Place on a cookie sheet and bake 30 minutes at 325 degrees.

LENTIL RICE PATTIES

2	c. cooked lentils		salt as needed
2	c. cooked brown rice	1	c. crumbs
½	onion, chopped		nut milk to moisten
1	tsp. sage		if needed

Mix together. Place on cookie sheet. Bake 20 minutes at 350 degrees.

MEATLESS HAMBURGERS

1	c. walnuts, chopped	½	tsp. sage
1	c. blended olives	½	tsp. thyme
2	c. rolled oats	¼	tsp. marjoram
1	chopped onion	2	c. nut milk
1	tsp. salt	½	tsp. garlic powder
1	Tbsp. soy sauce	½	tsp. onion salt

Mix together all ingredients. Let stand 15 to 20 minutes. Form into patties and brown about 15 minutes on each side in skillet over medium heat, or in oven for 30 minutes at 325 degrees.

MILLET PATTIES - 1

Blend:

| ½ | c. raw cashews | 1 | c. hot water |

Add and mix well:

1½	c. cooked millet	½	tsp. garlic powder
½	c. whl. wheat flour	1	Tbsp. soy sauce
¼	c. soy flour		salt to taste
½	c. chopped onion		

Form patties and bake 30 minutes at 325 degrees.

MILLET PATTIES - 2

Blend:

2	c. hot water	1	c. raw cashews
1	onion		

Add:

3	c. cooked millet	1	c. cornmeal
½	c. soy flour	1	tsp. sage
½	tsp. garlic powder	1	tsp. salt

Form patties and bake on cookie sheets 30 minutes at 325 degrees. Turn once.

OATMEAL - WHEAT GERM PATTIES

1½	c. uncooked oatmeal		pinch of sage
1	c. wheat germ		dash of garlic powder
1	pkg. dry yeast in ¼ c.	1	chopped onion
	water or 1 Tbsp. dry yeast	8	tsp. soy flour, with 8 tsp.
4	tsp. soy sauce		water
1	tsp. salt	¼	c. chopped nuts
1½	c. nut milk		

Dissolve yeast in water and mix all ingredients together. Form into patties and bake on Pam sprayed cookie sheet in a 350 degree oven until brown, 20 to 30 minutes.

Place patties in casserole dish and cover with favorite brown gravy or onion gravy and bake for 45 minutes at 350 degrees.

SAVORY SOYBEAN PATTIES

3	c. water	1	tsp. Ital. herb seasoning
⅔	c. dry soybeans	2	Tbsp. soy sauce
1¼	c. water	½	tsp. salt
1⅓	c. rolled oats	1	Tbsp. Brewer's type yeast
1	small chopped onion or		(optional)
1	tsp. onion powder		

Soak soybeans overnight in 3 cups water. Drain. Blend soybeans in 1¼ cups water until quite fine.

Remove to bowl and add seasonings and rolled oats. Allow to stand 10 minutes for rolled oats to absorb moisture. Stir again and drop by rounded tablespoons on cookie sheet.

Cook until lightly browned. Turn and cook until lightly browned. Reduce heat to 275 degrees and allow to cook 10 minutes longer.

Serve with tomato gravy.

Bake at 325 degrees.

SPROUTED WHEAT BURGERS

2	c. sprouted wheat	2	Tbsp. peanut butter
½	c. sunflower seeds, grd. or chopped	2	Tbsp. soy sauce
		1	Tbsp. onion powder or
½	c. pumpkin seeds, grd. or chopped	¼	c. chopped raw onion
		½	tsp. ea. of thyme, salt, and sage
2	c. cooked barley or millet		
½	c. soft bread crumbs		

Mold with hands to form patties. Brown on both sides. Place between burger buns and serve with homemade catsup. Or serve with gravy as a meatless main dish.

Bake in oven at 325 degrees for 30 minutes.

VEGEBURGERS

Cook and grind:

4	c. soybeans	2	c. garbanzos

Add:

3	c. cooked brown rice	2	Tbsp. chicken-style seasoning (McKay's)
2	onions, chopped		
1	Tbsp. sage	1	tsp. garlic powder
1	tsp. celery salt		

If dry, add bean stock. If wet, add crumbs or oatmeal.

Form patties and bake, covered with foil, for 25 minutes at 350 degrees, then turn and bake 10 minutes or more.

PICKLES

BEAN RELISH

Combine:

6	c. cooked red beans	2	cans corn with liquid

Set aside.

In a saucepan, combine:

½	c. dates	3	onions, chopped
1	c. water	1	tsp. salt
½	c. lemon juice	2	tsp. celery seed

Cook until onions are tender. Thicken with cornstarch and pour over beans and corn.

Chill 4 hours or overnight.

BREAD AND BUTTER PICKLES

Let stand 4 hours:

4	quarts thinly sliced unpeeled cucumbers	1	quart sliced onions
		½	c. salt

Drain well.

In large kettle, combine:

2	lg. cans pineapple juice	2	Tbsp. celery salt
2	c. lemon juice	1	Tbsp. dill seed
1	tsp. turmeric	4	cloves garlic

Bring juices to a boil and add cucumbers, onions, and heat.

Put in hot, clean jars and water bath in canner for 5 minutes.

DILLS

Boil and cool 16 cups of water and 1 cup salt. Set aside to cool. Soak cucumbers in plain cold water overnight. Scrub with a brush and soak 1 hour more in clean water.

Pack cucumbers in quart jars with 3 garlic cloves, sliced, 1 head fresh dill, and 3 carrot sticks.

Add salt water and seal. Leave in a warm room for at least 3 weeks before using.

PICKLED VEGETABLES

Cook until just tender, vegetables such as beets, carrots, turnips, cauliflower, or broccoli.

Put beets alone, but other vegetables can be combined. Also you can add raw cucumbers, zucchini, and onion rings one hour before serving.

Cover vegetables with the following:

12	oz. apple juice conc.	1	clove garlic
¾	c. lemon juice	1	tsp. ea. of dill and celery seed
1	c. hot water		

Chill several hours.

Write your extra recipes here:

SALADS

A B C SALAD

4	large apples, diced	1	c. celery, finely chopped
2	bananas, diced		or sliced

Add Coleslaw Dressing.

AVOCADO SALAD

¼	c. lemon juice	1	small head cauliflower,
2	large avocados, cubed		coarsely grated
4	green onions, sliced		

BEAN KRAUT SALAD

kidney beans	black olives
garbanzo beans	green peppers
onion rings	sauerkraut

Combine; eat as is or put on greens if you wish.

BEAN SLAW

½	medium head cabbage, shredded	1½	c. red beans

Use Coleslaw Dressing.

BROCCOLI SALAD

This broccoli dish can be either vegetable or salad on your menu.

1½	lbs. broccoli	2	Tbsp. minced green onion
	boiling, salted water	¼	tsp. garlic salt
3	Tbsp. lemon juice		sliced radishes for garnish

Trim off broccoli stem ends and peel outer layer of stalks; cut large spears in half lengthwise. Wash spears well.

Immerse in boiling, salted water and cook, uncovered, until just tender when pierced. Drain well; chill up to 24 hours.

For the dressing, combine the lemon juice, green onion, garlic salt, in a small jar; shake well.

About an hour before serving, arrange chilled broccoli spears on 6 lettuce-lined salad plates. Spoon dressing evenly over each; garnish with the radishes.

BRUSSELS SPROUTS SALAD

Put Coleslaw Dressing on hot cooked Brussels sprouts. Chill several hours. Add cherry tomatoes and sliced green onions just before serving.

CABBAGE

4	c. shredded cabbage	½	c. finely chopped onion
1½	c. whl. kernel corn	1	c. chopped olives

Add Coleslaw Dressing.

CRISPY SPROUTS SALAD

2	c. bean sprouts	½	c. fresh or fzn. grn. peas
2	c. alfalfa sprouts	1	c. raw mushrooms, sliced (optional)

Mix; serve with Avocado Dressing.

CUCUMBER SALAD

Overgrown, seedy cucumbers may be cut in half lengthwise and seeds scooped out. Fill centers with finely shredded cabbage or carrots or beets or a combination of vegetables mixed with Lemon Dressing.

FRUIT SALAD

Mix in a pretty bowl:

2	cut up oranges	3	sliced bananas
2	chopped apples	1	can unsweet. pineapple chunks with the juice
1	c. grapes		
2	c. strawberries, cut in ½		

No dressing needed.

GARBANZO - PINEAPPLE SALAD

3   c. cooked garbanzo   10   cherry tomatoes
    beans   1   can pineapple chunks
                                       with juice
Use French Dressing.

GREEN BEAN SALAD

Combine:

green beans   cherry tomatoes
onion rings

Add Italian Dressing and mix.

GREEN AND GOLD SALAD

3   c. shredded zucchini   ½   c. sliced green onions
3   c. shredded carrots
Blend and add:

¼   c. lemon juice   ½   c. dates
¼   c. hot water   salt as needed

GREEN PEA SALAD

1   c. sliced celery   3   c. cooked green peas
10 cherry tomatoes, cut in
    half
Use Tomato Dressing.

HOLIDAY SALAD BOWL

This salad could double as the vegetable for a holiday buffet.

1   lb. green beans   16 to18 cherry tomatoes,
    water   halved
1   can (6 or 8 oz.) water   ½   tsp. dry basil
    chestnuts, drained   ¼   tsp. ea. of oregano leaves
½   lb. mushrooms   and grated lemon peel
1   can (8 oz.) ripe olives,   2   tsp. lemon juice
    drained   garlic salt

Break off tips from beans; snap into about 2 inch lengths. Bring ½ inch water to a boil in a frying pan with a lid. Add beans, cover, and boil until just tender to bite, 5 to 7 minutes. Drain, plunge into cold water, drain again. Turn into a salad bowl.

Slice water chestnuts and mushrooms; add to beans along with olives and tomatoes. Add basil, oregano, and lemon peel and juice; pour over vegetables and mix well. Season with garlic salt to taste.

Cover and chill as long as overnight.

LETTUCE TOMATO SALAD

Blend:

2	c. raw cashews	½	c. chopped radishes
1	c. water	½	c. shredded carrot
2	Tbsp. parsley	½	tsp. garlic salt
½	c. sliced green onions	½	tsp. dill seed
⅓	c. celery or	1	tsp. turmeric
	1 Tbsp. celery seed		

Chill several hours and serve on green lettuce leaves and tomato slices.

LIMA BEAN SALAD

2	c. cooked green limas	2	c. cooked green peas
1	c. chopped celery		

Dressing:

1½	c. pineapple juice	1	tsp. onion powder
2	Tbsp. lemon juice	1	tsp. celery salt

MACARONI SALAD

3	c. cooked macaroni	1	c. sliced green onions
1	c. chopped ripe olives	2	c. whl. kernel corn
2	lg. tomatoes, chopped	1	c. green peas
2	c. garbanzo beans		

Use Coleslaw Dressing.

MAIN COURSE SALAD

3	c. torn salad greens	2	Tbsp. wheat germ

1	carrot, thinly sliced or	2	Tbsp. sunflower seeds
	coarsely grated	1	avocado, cubed
½	c. chopped peanuts	1	c. chopped radishes
3	Tbsp. chopped parsley		onion rings

Use Cucumber Dressing.

MANY BEAN SALAD

Use several beans (such as northern, garbanzo, red, plus whole string green and wax beans). Green pepper rings and onion rings, (white and red) are optional. A sprinkle of fresh lemon juice and salt is enough dressing.

MINT - AVOCADO SALAD

Mix:

½	c. cashew cream	2	Tbsp. lemon juice
3	Tbsp. fresh mint, finely	1	tsp. salt
	chopped		

Add to:

3	large avocados (cut in	2	bananas, sliced
	chunks)	1	can pineapple chunks,
			with juice

MOCK CRAB SALAD

Grind:

2	c. raw parsnips	½	c. raw onions
1	c. raw carrots	10	ripe olives

Moisten with Golden Sauce and serve on salad greens.

PEANUT, CARROT, RICE SALAD

Blend:

½	c. peanut butter	½	c. dates
½	c. hot water		

Add:

4	c. cooked brown rice	2	c. shredded carrots

Serve on lettuce.

POTATO SALAD

| 6 | cooked cubed potatoes | 1 | med. cucumber, thinly |
| 1 | small onion, thinly sliced | | sliced |

Dressing:

1	c. water	½	c. cashews
1	Tbsp. chicken-style seasoning (McKay's)	1	Tbsp. lemon juice salt as needed
1	tsp. dill seed		

Blend dressing ingredients; mix lightly and chill several hours.

RICE SALAD

Combine:

| 2 | c. cooked brown rice | ½ | c. chopped green onions |
| ½ | c. shredded carrot | ½ | c. diced cucumber |

Dressing:

Blend:

| ¼ | c. lemon juice | ½ | tsp. salt |
| ¼ | c. water | 4 | dates |

Serve on lettuce leaves and top with sesame seeds.

ROSY CRUNCH SALAD

1	c. shredded raw carrots	¼	c. sunflower seeds
1	c. shredded raw beets		green pepper strips
1	c. shredded raw turnips		endive or leaf lettuce

Toss all shredded vegetables together with Italian Dressing and sunflower seeds.

Serve on bed of endive or lettuce. Garnish with green pepper strips.

SPINACH SALAD

Combine:

fresh shredded spinach	thinly sliced zucchini
broken lettuce	thinly sliced celery
thinly sliced carrot	

Use Sweet Basil Dressing.

"6" THINGS SALAD

Mix in a bowl:

3	c. torn lettuce	1	c. cooked or fresh peas
1	c. sliced black olives	½	c. sliced green onion
1	c. cooked brown rice	10	cherry tomatoes, cut in half

Use Italian Dressing.

SPRING VEGETABLE SALAD

Cook separately until just tender:

    tiny whole potatoes   asparagus spears
    whole green beans   fresh peas

Line a salad bowl with lettuce leaves and arrange the above vegetables over them.

Add:

    garbanzo beans   tomato wedges
    onion rings   olives

Cover and cool several hours.

Serve with Avocado Dressing.

TOMATO ASPIC

Combine:

4	Tbsp. cornstarch	2	Tbsp. lemon juice
¾	tsp. onion salt		

Gradually add 2 cups tomato juice. Boil 2 minutes, stirring constantly. Pour in mold and refrigerate.

May add celery or olives (sliced thinly).

VEGETABLE SALAD

1	quart chopped lettuce	10	radishes, thinly sliced
3	diced tomatoes	¼	c. chopped fresh parsley
1	cucumber, thinly sliced	¼	c. chopped fresh mint
5	green onions, thinly sliced		

Dressing:

Blend:

½	c. lemon juice	6	dates
¼	c. water	¼	tsp. garlic salt or
			1 clove fresh, finely grated

WHITE BEAN SALAD

Blend:

½	c. lemon juice	1	tsp. salt
½	c. hot water	1	medium size onion
6	dates	½	c. raw cashews

Pour over 4 cups cooked hot white beans. Cool several hours.

Add:

½	c. chopped fresh parsley	1	c. sliced radishes

Serve.

ZIPPY SPINACH TOSS

1	bunch spinach, washed thoroughly	¼	lb. fresh mushrooms, washed and sliced
6	cauliflower flowerettes, thinly sliced		

Tear spinach into bite-sized pieces, discarding stems. Toss all ingredients.

For variation, add 1 small sweet red onion, thinly sliced, sliced radishes, carrots or olives.

SALAD DRESSING

AVOCADO - CASHEW DRESSING

Blend until smooth:

½ c. raw cashews	1½ c. hot water

Add and continue to blend:

2 avocados	2 tsp. lemon juice

Cool before using.

For dip, add ½ medium size onion to first ingredients.

AVOCADO DRESSING

½ c. orange juice	¼ tsp. salt
1 Tbsp. lemon juice	1 avocado, mashed

COLESLAW DRESSING

1 c. raw cashews	1 tsp. salt
3 c. pineapple juice	1 tsp. onion powder
⅓ c. lemon juice	

Blend.

CUCUMBER DRESSING

Blend until smooth:

¾ c. raw cashews	4 thick slices cucumber
¾ c. hot water	4 green onions

Cool.

Add before using:

¼ c. minced parsley	1 tsp. salt and herbs your
¼ c. diced radishes	family likes

DRESSING FOR SALADS
OR COOKED VEGETABLES

Blend:

2 fresh tomatoes

or 2 raw carrots   or 1 cucumber
or 10 radishes   or 1 seeded green pepper
¼ c. water

Add:

onion powder   garlic powder
celery salt   lemon juice

to taste

FRENCH DRESSING

½ c. lemon juice   ½ tsp. paprika
½ tsp. salt   ⅓ c. water
¼ c. raw cashews   garlic, onion and dill as desired

Blend.

ITALIAN DRESSING

⅓ c. lemon juice   1 tsp. crushed basil
3 c. pineapple juice   1 tsp. onion powder
1 tsp. celery seed

Mix well and shake before using.

LEMON DRESSING

Blend.

2 Tbsp. grated lemon peel   ½ tsp. cumin
½ c. lemon juice   ½ tsp. paprika
2 cloves garlic, fine grated   ½ tsp. turmeric
1 c. tomato juice   6 dates
½ tsp. coriander

MAYONNAISE (Or Use As Sour Cream)

Thicken 2 cups water with 3 tablespoons cornstarch. Cool slightly.

Blend well:

2 c. hot water   2 c. raw cashews

Add and blend well:

¾ c. lemon juice   2 tsp. garlic powder

1 Tbsp. salt	2 tsp. onion powder

Add to the starch mixture and mix thoroughly. Cool before using.

MOCK MAYONNAISE

Blend:

1½ c. water	½ c. unbleached white flour

Cook over medium heat until thick and bubbly. Cool.

Return to blender and add:

2 Tbsp. lemon juice	1 tsp. salt
6 dates	⅛ tsp. garlic powder
⅛ tsp. onion powder	

Blend until creamy. Store in covered container in refrigerator.

Variation: For more zip, add few shakes dill weed, paprika, turmeric or other herbs.

SWEET BASIL DRESSING

2 Tbsp. dry onion	1 tsp. sweet basil
1 c. hot water	2 Tbsp. lemon juice
½ c. raw cashews	10 olives
½ tsp. salt	

Blend.

TOMATO - CASHEW DRESSING

½ c. raw cashews	1 tsp. marjoram
½ raw onion	2 c. tomato juice
1 tsp. garlic powder	6 oz. apple juice conc.
1 tsp. celery salt	salt if needed
1 tsp. paprika	

Blend well.

TOMATO DRESSING

½ c. tomato juice	1 tsp. dried parsley
2 Tbsp. lemon juice	1 tsp. food yeast
1 tsp. onion powder	

Put in a jar and shake before using.

Write an extra recipe here:

SAUCES

CASHEW CHEESE

1	c. water	1	Tbsp. agar flakes

Cook together until clear, 2 or 3 minutes. Pour hot into blender. Add:

1½	c. raw cashews	½	tsp. onion powder
1	tsp. salt		small amount of carrot (for color)

Blend well; add ¼ cup lemon juice.

Store in refrigerator.

CASHEW CHEESE SPREAD

1	c. raw cashews	½	tsp. onion powder
½	c. hot water	¼	c. lemon juice
½	tsp. salt	1	can (2 oz.) pimentos or
½	tsp. garlic powder		1 carrot, sliced (for color)

Blend.

CATSUP

Blend:

1	small onion	1	c. tomato sauce
1	tsp. garlic powder	8	dates
¼	c. lemon juice		

Add:

1	c. tomato sauce	1	tsp. paprika
1	c. tomato paste	½	tsp. cumin
1	tsp. salt	½	tsp. basil

Simmer for 1 hour, stirring occasionally.

GOLDEN SAUCE

Blend:

1	c. cooked, diced potato	1	c. water (from cooked vegetables)
1	large cooked carrot		

½ c. raw cashews
1 tsp. onion or celery salt
¼ c. lemon juice

This is good on cauliflower, broccoli, *etc.*

NUTEENA - LIKE SANDWICH SPREAD

1¼ c. garbanzo beans, cooked, reserve liquid
⅔ c. chopped olives
⅓ c. garbanzo liquid
⅓ c. peanut butter

1½ Tbsp. tomato paste
¾ tsp. Brewer's yeast
1/16 tsp. onion powder
1/16 tsp. lemon juice

Mash garbanzo beans thoroughly. *Mash* in remaining ingredients.

PARMESAN CHEESE

Blend:

1 c. sesame seeds
¼ c. lemon juice

Add and mix:

1 c. Brewer's yeast flakes
1 Tbsp. onion powder
¼ c. Bakon yeast

2 tsp. garlic powder
3 Tbsp. chicken-style seasoning (McKay's)

Store in a covered container in a cool place.

SAUCE FOR GREENS (MUSTARD)

Combine and heat:

½ tsp. thyme
2 tsp. vegesalt
1 tsp. turmeric

⅓ c. lemon juice
1 c. water
2 Tbsp. cornstarch

Serve on any greens. For mustard let the above cool a little and blend with 1 cup raw cashews.

Use as dressing or dip.

SOYBEAN SPREAD

2 c. cooked soybeans
3 Tbsp. parsley
2 Tbsp. dried onion

1 clove garlic
salt as needed

Blend.

SPANISH SAUCE

Cook:

4	c. coarse chopped onions	3	c. sliced celery
1	c. water		

Add and heat:

1	c. sliced mushrooms	½	Tbsp. chicken-style
1	c. sliced ripe olives		seasoning (McKay's)
1	c. ckd. mshd. tomatoes	½	tsp. garlic powder
½	tsp. oregano	1	tsp. cumin
2	c. tomato paste		

Use on rice, beans, barley, or pasta.

Write your extra recipes here:

SOUPS AND STEWS

AUTUMN VEGETABLE CHOWDER

1	c. water	1	can (1 lb.) tomatoes
1	med. sz. onion, chopped	1	Tbsp. beef style
1	c. thinly sliced carrot		seasoning (McKay's)
½	c. thinly sliced celery	2	c. nut milk
2	c. peeled, diced potatoes		salt
	chopped parsley		

In a 3 quart pan, put water and the onion; cook until limp. Stir in the carrot, celery, potatoes, tomatoes and seasoning. Cover and simmer for 35 minutes, stirring occasionally, or until vegetables are tender when pierced. Gradually stir in milk and heat until piping hot; season to taste with salt.

Ladle into mugs or small bowls; sprinkle with parsley.

BEAN SOUP OR STEW

Soak and cook 1 cup dry lima beans, lentils, navy beans, or garbanzo beans until done.

For soup, cut the vegetables small - for stew, use whole vegetables, or cut in chunks.

Cook until tender:

2	c. carrots	2	medium size potatoes
2	medium size onions	1½	quarts tomato juice

Combine vegetables and beans and 2 cups peas.

Heat and serve.

BLACK BEANS OVER RICE

1	lb. black beans	1	bay leaf
1	large onion, chopped	2	tsp. salt
2	green peppers, chopped	1	lb. brown rice, cooked
1	clove garlic, minced		green onions, chopped

Cover beans with 6 cups boiling water and let set 1 hour. Drain and add 6 cups fresh cold water. Cook over low heat (gently bubbling) 1 hour. Saute onions, green peppers and garlic in ¼ cup water. Combine with beans; add other seasonings and cook until beans are tender and liquid is thick.

Serve over brown rice and top with green onions.

BORSCH

Cook until tender:

5	stalks celery, sliced	½	tsp. ea. of thyme, sage
2	heads cabbage, sliced		marjoram
2	c. diced onions	2	Tbsp. chicken-style
1	c. sliced carrots		seasoning (McKay's)
1	tsp. garlic powder	2	Tbsp. lemon juice
1	quart water		

Blend:

2	c. cooked beets	1	quart water

Add to cooked vegetables; heat and serve.

CHILI

6	c. cooked chili or pinto beans	3	c. tomato juice
		1	tsp. garlic powder
1	c. tomato paste	2	tsp. cumin

Salt, if needed. Simmer 1 hour.

CHILLED GREEN BEAN BISQUE

⅓	c. slivered almonds	2	c. water
1	clove garlic, minced or pressed	4	c. green beans, in 1 inch pieces (about 1 lb.)
1	med. sz. onion, chopped vegesalt to taste	¼	tsp. savory leaves

Toast almonds in a 350 degree oven for 5 to 7 minutes, or until golden; set aside. Put ¼ cup water in a 3 quart pan, over medium heat; add garlic and onion and saute until limp. Stir in beans and water; cover and simmer 10 minutes, or until beans are tender to bite. Turn mixture into a blender and whirl until smooth; season with savory and salt. Cover and chill well.

To serve, pour into chilled mugs, then top each with nuts.

CORN CHOWDER

Cook:

2	c. thawed, fzn. or canned corn	1	c. grated cooked potato
1	Tbsp. chicken-style seasoning (McKay's)	2	c. water
		1	tsp. sweet basil

Add blended:

2	c. hot water		salt if needed
1	c. raw cashews		

Heat and serve.

CREAMY HERBED WALNUT SOUP

1½	c. chopped walnuts	½	c. thinly sliced celery
	water	1	med. sz. onion, sliced
2	c. cashew milk	2	Tbsp. all-purpose flour
½	bay leaf	3	c. chicken flavored broth (McKay's)
¼	tsp. ea. of thyme leaves and dry basil	¼	c. water
2	Tbsp. chopped parsley		finely chopped chives or green onion

Cover walnuts with water and bring to a boil; boil for 3 minutes then drain. Pour milk over drained nuts and add bay leaf, thyme, basil, and parsley; heat, but do not boil; cover and set aside for 20 minutes.

Meanwhile, in a 3 quart pan, combine water, onion and celery, and cook about 5 minutes. Blend in the flour and broth; cook, stirring, until soup boils. Reduce heat and simmer gently for 10 minutes, then remove bay leaf and add milk mixture to soup. Whirl soup a small amount at a time in a blender until pureed.

Cover and refrigerate if made ahead.

Just before serving, reheat to simmering. Sprinkle each serving with chives.

GARBANZOS - ALMONDS

Marinate 2 cups cooked garbanzos in ⅓ cup soy sauce and ⅔ cup water overnight.

Combine and cook briefly.

1½	c. finely sliced celery	1	pkg. Chinese pea pods
1	c. chopped onions	2	chopped tomatoes
1	can bamboo shoots	1	Tbsp. chicken-style
1	can sliced wtr. chestnuts		seasoning (McKay's)
1	c. water		

Add drained garbanzos, thicken slightly with cornstarch.
Serve over rice and sprinkle with chopped almonds.

GARBANZO SOUP

Blend:

2	c. cooked garbanzos	½	c. lemon juice
1	tsp. salt	1	c. sesame seeds
½	tsp. garlic salt or fresh garlic	2	c. water

Serve chilled.

ICY LEMON SOUP

Blend to make cashew cream:

1	c. raw cashews	2	c. water

Add:

1	c. water	¾	c. lemon juice
1	Tbsp. curry *		

Cool several hours and serve with thin lemon slices.

* Curry:

2	Tbsp. turmeric	3	bay leaves
2	Tbsp. cumin	¼	tsp. garlic powder
1	Tbsp. coriander	½	tsp. onion powder

Grind in Moulinex.

LENTIL - RICE SOUP

½	c. brown rice	1	lg. can tomatoes
1	c. lentils, dry	1 to 1½	tsp. salt to taste
2	quarts water	2	Tbsp. soy sauce
1	large onion, chopped		

Mix and cook slowly until all ingredients are tender. Sometimes more liquid is needed. Add tomato juice for more liquid. Thyme or oregano may be added.

LENTIL LEMON SOUP

1½	c. washed lentils	2	Tbsp. chicken-style
7	c. cold water		seasoning (McKay's)
1	tsp. coriander	1	med. size chopped onion
3	cloves garlic, grated fine		

Bring to simmer; add:

1	large raw, diced potato, unpeeled	1½	lbs. chopped greens

Cook 30 minutes.

Add:

3	Tbsp. lemon juice	½	tsp. cumin

Serve topped with thin lemon slices.

MINESTRONE

Cook until macaroni is done.

3	c. water	1	carrot, coarse grated
1	c. chopped onion	¼	tsp. thyme
¾	c. chopped celery	¼	tsp. savory
2	c. chopped tomatoes	½	tsp. garlic powder
2	small zucchini, sliced	1	c. whl. wheat macaroni

Add 2 cups cooked garbanzos, 1 quart of water and chicken-style (McKay's) flavored seasoning to taste.

MUSHROOM SOUP

Saute 15 minutes in a small amount of water:

1	c. chopped onions	2	c. diced fresh mushrooms

Add:

1	c. water	1	tsp. chicken-style seasoning (McKay's)

Blend this until very smooth.

Cook until the potatoes are done:

3	c. fine diced raw potatoes	1	Tbsp. chicken-style
4	c. water		seasoning (McKay's)
3	c. sliced fresh mushrooms		

Combine both above mixtures and add ¼ teaspoon paprika, ¼ cup dried parsley or ½ cup fresh parsley.

Blend and add:

1½	c. hot water	1	c. cashews

Simmer (do not boil) and serve.

MUSHROOM - PEA SAUCE (For Pasta or Grain)

Cook until onions are limp:

4	lg. onions, sliced	¼	c. water

Add:

1	c. sliced mushrooms	1	clove garlic, minced

Cook until mushrooms are tender.

Just before serving, add 2 packages (20 ounces) frozen peas.

Heat and serve.

PARSNIP SOUP

Cook 15 minutes until parsnips are soft and then blend:

2	lbs. peeled and thinly sliced parsnips	3	c. water
1	large diced onion	2	Tbsp. chicken-style seasoning (McKay's)

Blend. Then add:

1	c. raw cashews	1	c. hot water

Combine, heat, and serve.

POTATO SOUP

Saute:

1	lg. onion, chopped	¼	c. water

Add:

3	c. water	½	tsp. dill seed

1	pkg. (10 oz.) fzn. mixed vegetables	2	Tbsp. chicken-style seasoning (McKay's)
3	potatoes, unpeeled, diced		

Simmer 25 minutes. Add:

2	c. nut cream	½	tsp. garlic salt

Heat and serve.

RICE SOUP

Heat to boiling:

6	c. water	3	Tbsp. chicken-style seasoning (McKay's)

Add:

½	c. chopped onion	½	c. chopped carrot
1	c. chopped celery	1	c. raw brown rice.

Simmer until rice is done, about 45 minutes.

SPINACH SOUP

Serve over rice or millet or spaghetti.

1	c. water	1	tsp. celery seed
2	med. sz. chopped onions	½	tsp. garlic salt
1	tsp. oregano		

Cook until done. Add 2 packages frozen chopped spinach or other greens, or equal amount fresh greens.

Cook briefly, only until hot.

TOMATO - RICE OR BARLEY SOUP

Cook until done:

6	c. tomato juice	1½	c. diced onions
2	c. diced celery	1	tsp. celery salt

Add 2½ cups cooked brown rice or barley.

TOMATO SOUP

Heat to boiling:

4	6 oz. cans tomato juice	¼	c. lemon juice

1	tsp. celery seed	¼	c. parsley
¼	tsp. cumin	¼	c. diced or grated onion
½	tsp. sweet basil	1	Tbsp. soy sauce

For cream of tomato, remove from heat and add cashew cream, made by blending 2 cups hot water and 1 cup raw cashews until smooth.

TOMATO STEW

Cook until tender:

6	med. sz. potatoes, cubed	1	c. diced onions

Add and heat only, 2½ cups fresh or canned chopped tomatoes. Salt, if needed.

VEGETABLE BISQUE

Cook until tender:

1½	c. diced carrots	3½	c. water
2	c. sliced leeks or onions	2	Tbsp. chicken-style
2	c. diced raw potatoes		seasoning (McKay's)

Add 1 cup watercress. Cook 2 minutes. Blend ingredients and add 1 cup cashew milk.

Serve cold with thinly sliced raw green onions and croutons.

VEGETABLE SOUP (3 Ways)

Cook until tender:

4	coarse chopped onions	4	parsnips, sliced thinly
4	sliced carrots	1	c. chopped parsley
4	stalks celery with leaves, sliced	½	tsp. ea. of thyme & basil salt if needed
2	c. green beans	3	quarts water

A. Drain for broth.
B. Eat as is.
C. Blend.

TOFU DISHES

TOFU

Be sure the tofu is fresh and drain several hours before using.

COOL SLAW

Combine:

1	c. grated carrots	⅔	c. sunflower seeds
2	c. shredded cabbage	1	c. diced celery
½	c. chopped peanuts		

Dressing:

Blend.

1	c. tofu	8	dates
¼	c. lemon juice	¼	c. water

FONDU SAUCE FOR VEGETABLES

2	c. water	½	c. raw cashews
1	large potato	¼	c. flaked yeast
1	carrot	2	tsp. paprika
1	onion	½	c. lemon juice
1	tofu brick (1 lb.)	2½	tsp. salt
	pinch of garlic powder		

Use 1 cup water to cook vegetables (cut fine). Add 1 cup water, lemon juice, cashews; blend. Then add seasonings to the vegetables.

Last, add tofu, blending well.

Makes about 7 cups.

TOFU LASAGNE

Tomato Sauce:

½	c. chopped onion	½	tsp. oregano
½	c. chopped celery	½	tsp. sweet basil
¼	c. chopped green pepper	½	tsp. salt
½	c. shredded carrots	1	quart blended tomatoes
1	clove minced garlic		

Combine ingredients for sauce and simmer 1 hour.

Cook lasagne noodles until tender. Drain 1 block tofu by crumbling into colander. Mix tofu with the following cashew cheese:

Cashew Cheese:

1	**c. water**	**1**	**tsp. salt**
1	**c. raw cashews**	**¼**	**c. lemon juice**
3	**Tbsp. Brewer's yeast**	**1**	**small jar pimentos, or**
½	**tsp. ea. of onion and**		**some canned tomato for**
	garlic salt		**color**

Liquefy all.

In large oblong Pyrex dish, layer noodles, sauce and then tofu-cheese mixture. Repeat, using 3 layers of noodles. Drizzle top with some reserved cashew cheese.

Bake.

TOFU MAYONNAISE

May be used as sauce on baked potato, green salad or on bread.

1	**pound tofu**	**2**	**tsp. salt**
2	**c. cooked garbanzos**	**2**	**Tbsp. lemon juice**
½	**c. cashews**	**½**	**c. sesame seeds**

Add liquid from garbanzos and enough water to equal 2 cups and 1 clove garlic. Blend.

TOFU AND MUSHROOMS

Blend and cook until thickened.

1	**c. hot water**	**10**	**dates**
¼	**c. soy sauce**	**1½**	**Tbsp. cornstarch**

Simmer 8 minutes.

2	**c. mushrooms**	**1**	**lb. tofu, drained and cut**
1	**c. chopped green onions**		**in 1 inch cubes**
		½	**c. water**

Add sauce and serve.

TOFU PATTIES

1½	**c. mashed garbanzos**	**2**	**c. diced fresh bread**
1	**lb. tofu, crumbled**		**crumbs**

Blend and add:

1	med. size onion	1½	c. olives
¼	c. water	2	Tbsp. chicken-style seasoning (McKay's)

Mix well and drop by spoonfuls on Pam-sprayed cookie sheets. Bake for 1 hour at 300 degrees.

PEANUT TOFU

Blend:

½	c. peanut butter	½	c. water
¼	c. lemon juice	10	dates

Pour over:

2	c. pineapple chunks	1	c. chopped peanuts
1	c. sliced water chestnuts	2	bananas, sliced
1	lb. tofu, cut in cubes		

SALAD

Combine:

2	cucumbers, ¼-ed and sliced in ½ inch chunks	1	small onion, diced

Blend and use as a dressing:

¼	c. water	¼	tsp. cumin
¼	c. lemon juice	½	tsp. salt
½	c. tofu	6	dates

TOFU SMOOTHIE DRINK

Blend:

6	oz. tofu (soft)	1	c. strawberries
1	c. apple juice	6	dates
2	bananas	1	tsp. vanilla

TOFU (SOUR) SOUP

Bring to a boil:

4	c. water	2	Tbsp. lemon juice

1	Tbsp. chicken-style seasoning (McKay's)	4	oz. tomato sauce
		1	Tbsp. soy sauce

Add:

½	lb. tofu, crumbled	½	c. sliced water chestnuts
1	c. canned sliced mushrooms (optional)	2	c. cooked brown rice

Bring to boil and add:

2	Tbsp. cornstarch	3	Tbsp. cold water

Serve topped with finely diced scallions or chives.

TOFU (Homemade)

Blend:

4	c. water	½	c. whl. wheat flour
2¼	c. soy flour	⅓	c. lemon juice
⅔	c. pimentos	½	tsp. garlic salt
1	Tbsp. salt	1	Tbsp. food yeast

Pour in a loaf pan and bake 2 hours at 275 degrees. Turn off oven heat, but keep tofu in oven 1 more hour.

Slice or crumble or cube for serving.

Write an extra recipe here:

VEGETABLES.

ACORN SQUASH

Fill cavity with bread dressing. Wrap in foil.
Bake for 1 hour at 350 degrees.

ASPARAGUS

Boiling tied in bunches, stalks down, saves mangling the tops.
Good served hot or cold. May use Golden Sauce.

BROCCOLI

Watch carefully to keep bright color. Do not overcook. Using flat
pan, as electric skillet, means one layer, little water and broccoli
cooks in less than 5 minutes. Lift cover often to keep color.

BRUSSELS SPROUTS AND CORN

Combine and cook Brussels sprouts, whole kernel corn, sliced
water chestnuts or mushrooms in salted water.

BEETS

Cook tiny beets, tops and all. Small beets need only a little salt, or
add a little fresh lemon juice, if you wish.

BLENDER BORSCH

Blend well:

1	c. cashew cream	1	inch slice lemon w/peel
2	c. beets, diced	½	small onion
	salt		

Just before serving, add 1 cup chopped ice.
Blend briefly and serve at once.

PICKLED BEETS

2	tsp. lemon juice	1	tsp. salt
2	c. apple juice or pineapple juice		

Heat to boiling point and pour over 1 quart cooked beets. Let stand 48 hours. Liquid can be used more than once, or can be thickened for hot beets.

BEETS PIQUANT

Cook 1½ cups grated beets in water with juice of 2 oranges, grated peel of 1 orange, ½ teaspoons vega salt, juice of 1 lemon and ½ teaspoon cardamon.

When done, thicken with cornstarch.

CAULIFLOWER AND TOMATOES

Combine and cook cauliflower flowerettes, sliced zucchini and quartered tomatoes in small amount of water.

CAULIFLOWER AND DIP

Eat it raw or cook briefly; add Avocado Dip.

CREAM OF CAULIFLOWER

Cook and mash 1 head cauliflower, 3 medium potatoes, add salt, ¼ cup chopped parsley and ½ cup nut cream.

CABBAGE

Delicious raw. Cook briefly with poppy seeds, vega salt, and add ripe olives (chopped).

CABBAGE AND CORN

Combine and cook shredded cabbage and whole kernel corn in a small amount salted water.

CABBAGE AND VEGETABLES

Combine and cook green beans, onion rings, shredded cabbage and thinly sliced carrots in a small amount of salted water.

CABBAGE IN CREAM

Cook 2 pounds sliced cabbage in 1 cup water. Combine and add:

| 1 | Tbsp. cornstarch | ½ | c. nut cream |
| 4 | Tbsp. lemon juice | | salt and caraway seeds, as desired |

Heat briefly to thicken.

RED CABBAGE

Cook until done:

| 2 | lbs. sliced red cabbage | salt (it helps the cabbage |
| 1 | c. water | to keep its color) |

Combine and add and cook to thicken:

| 1 | Tbsp. cornstarch | 2 | Tbsp. lemon juice |

CABBAGE ROLLS

20   cabbage leaves, cooked until tender, or 1 head cabbage, sliced thin

Combine and cook briefly:

1	c. cooked navy beans	¼	c. parsley
1	c. finely diced onions	½	c. chopped celery
1	c. cooked rice	¼	c. chopped green pepper
1	c. chopped tomatoes	1	tsp. savory salt

Put a large spoonful in a cabbage leaf; roll up; place closely in cabbage leaf-lined baking pan.

Heat 15 to 20 minutes at 350 degrees.

Or cook sauce until nearly done. Add shredded cabbage on top and cook no more than 8 to 10 minutes.

CABBAGE SOUP

Cook until done:

1	c. diced onion	½	tsp. dill seed
3	med. size cubed potatoes	½	tsp. poppy seed
6	c. water	½	tsp. celery seed
	vegesalt to taste		

Add a few minutes before serving, 1 small head thinly sliced cabbage and 1 cup chopped parsley.

EGGPLANT

2   large eggplants, peeled, cubed, cooked in a little salted water-15 minutes and drained

Cook 45 minutes:

1	c. diced onion	**1**	c. raw brown rice
½	c. chopped parsley	**2**	c. water

Combine all ingredients plus 1 teaspoon Italian herbs and 1 cup bread crumbs. Two cups tomatoes, quartered.

Bake for 30 minutes at 350 degrees.

EGGPLANT BAKED

Peel and dice and cook in ½ cup salted water, 1 medium eggplant. Drain well.

Add:

1½	c. soft bread crumbs	**½**	c. nut milk
¼	tsp. marjoram	**½**	c. snipped parsley

Bake at 350 degrees for 30 minutes.

EGGPLANT BROILED

Brown slices of eggplant under the broiler. Put in a casserole and top with sliced green onions, garlic powder, tomato slices, lemon juice, sweet basil.

Bake 40 minutes at 350 degrees.

EGGPLANT CASSEROLE NUMBER 1

Peel and chop one large eggplant. Add:

1	c. finely diced onion	**1**	tsp. chicken-style seasoning (McKay's)
2	c. tomato juice		
1½	c. cooked millet or brown rice	**¼**	c. snipped parsley
		1	c. whl. kernel corn
1	tsp. cumin		

Bake at 350 degrees for 45 minutes.

EGGPLANT CASSEROLE NUMBER 2

1	lg. (about 1½ lbs.) eggplant	1	clove garlic, minced or pressed
⅓	c. water	1	lg. can (15 oz.) tomato sauce
1	med. size onion, chopped		
¼	lb. mushrooms, sliced	½	tsp. ea. of dry basil and oregano leaves
	salt to taste		

Cut eggplant into ½ inch thick slices; arrange in a single layer on a rimmed baking sheet.

Bake, uncovered, in a 450 degree oven until browned and very soft, about 30 minutes.

Heat ⅓ cup water in a frying pan over medium heat; add onion, mushrooms, and garlic and cook until soft. Add tomato sauce, basil, and oregano; simmer, uncovered, for 10 minutes. Season to taste with salt.

Layer about half the eggplant in a shallow 1½ quart casserole; top with half the sauce. Repeat layers.

Bake, uncovered, in a 350 degree oven, until hot and bubbly, about 25 minutes.

EGGPLANT CASSEROLE NUMBER 3

Cut 2 eggplants in ½ inch slices. Place on a cookie sheet and bake at 400 degrees for 30 minutes. Turn after 15 minutes.

Blend:

1½	c. tomato juice	¼	c. parsley
1	small onion	1	rib celery

Layer in a casserole the eggplant, the tomato mixture, bread crumbs and ground peanuts.

Bake for 20 minutes at 350 degrees.

EGGPLANT STUFFED

Cook 2 whole eggplants for 20 minutes in boiling water. Cool, drain, cut in half lengthwise, scoop out the pulp.

Filling:

	all the chopped pulp	¼	c. chopped parsley
½	c. finely diced onion	¼	c. chopped celery and
1	diced tomatoes		leaves
⅔	c. cooked brown rice	½	tsp. garlic salt

Mix and fill eggplants.

Bake for 15 minutes at 400 degrees.

GREENS

A. Cook 1 pound shredded *spinach* in 2 tablespoons soy sauce and ¼ cup water.

B. Cook 1 pound chopped *spinach*, 1 cup cooked brown rice, 2 tablespoons finely chopped onion, ¼ teaspoon thyme and ¾ cup nut milk.

C. *Swiss Chard:* This is a mild flavor green. Chop and cook only to wilt. Serve at once with sauce for greens.

GREEN CASSEROLE

Blend:

3	c. wilted spinach or other greens

Set aside.

Blend:

1½	c. any cooked legume	1½	c. water
1	Tbsp. beef-style seasoning (McKay's)		

Combine greens and beans.

Add:

2	c. fresh whl. wheat bread crumbs

Bake at 350 degrees for ½ hour.

GREEN PEAS

Cook peas only a few minutes in water, ⅛ teaspoon onion salt, ⅛ teaspoon garlic salt and ¼ teaspoon marjoram.

Tiny cooked onions can be added.

GREEN PEAS AND MINT

Serve peas with fresh snipped mint or dried mint and grated orange or lemon peel.

PEAS AND WHEAT

½   c. cooked whl. kernel wheat

1   pkg. fzn. peas (or most any other vegetable)

Serve hot.

GREEN PEA SOUP

Blend until smooth:

2   c. hot water
1   c. raw cashews
1   Tbsp. onion powder

¼   tsp. celery seed
1   tsp. salt (dash garlic and thyme)

Add and blend 1 pound fresh or frozen peas, 3 cups hot water. Heat, but do not boil; serve.

GREEN BEANS

A. Add very finely chopped raw onion and hot lemon juice just before serving.

B. Add water chestnuts or mushrooms.

C. Put small amount of Italian herbs in cooking water of fresh beans.

D. Cook beans; add quartered tomatoes and sliced zucchini and cook 8 minutes.

E. Add summer savory and parsley for flavor or thin onion rings are good, too.

GREEN BEANS CALIFORNIA

1   lg. sliced onion
1   qt. fresh green beans
½   c. water
1   tsp. vege salt

½   tsp. thyme
¼   tsp. oregano
¼   tsp. summer savory
¼   tsp. marjoram

Cooking time varies as to the maturity of the beans.

GREEN BEANS AND SEEDS

Cook:

1	lb. green beans	½	tsp. basil
½	c. water	1	tsp. vege salt
1	thinly sliced onion	¼	c. sunflower seeds

MUSHROOMS

Cook large fresh whole mushrooms slowly in small amounts-1 part soy sauce and 2 parts water-on griddle or frypan.

MUSHROOM ROAST

1	c. celery	1	can water chestnuts
1	lb. fresh mushrooms	1	c. cashew milk
1	c. chopped onions	1	c. cashew nuts
1	can mushrooms	2	c. cooked brown rice

Chop onions, celery, and mushrooms. Cook these three together in small amount of water until tender. Add all other ingredients.

Bake for 40 minutes at 300 degrees.

ONIONS AND BEANS

Put whole small onions in baked beans before baking.

ONIONS BAKED

Bake small onions, small carrots and 1 inch slant cut celery.

Add vege salt.

ONIONS BAKED WITH RICE

Peel 6 to 8 onions, slice crosswise, and steam until tender. Layer in baking dish with 2 cups cooked rice. Pour over contents-2 cups cashew milk seasoned with 1 teaspoon vegesalt. Put thin green pepper slices or whole green beans or green limas on top.

Bake at 350 degrees for 20 minutes.

ONIONS BOILED

Cook onion halves (cut side up) in one layer in frypan with water nearly to cover and a sprinkle of salt. Simmer about 30 minutes until done. Drain well and carefully.

Serve with paprika, chopped almond and snipped parsley.

ONIONS CREAMED

Cook together and then blend-2 pounds cubed potatoes and 2 pounds onions. Add:

1	Tbsp. tomato puree		salt
1	Tbsp. lemon juice	½	c. nut cream

Mix together.

POTATOES

Baked, boiled in jackets, riced or (?) potatoes with:

A. Paprika and parsley
B. Onion and garlic salt
C. Finely chopped green onion and grated lemon peel.
D. Hot cashew cream seasoned with chicken-style seasoning (McKay's) and onion powder

POTATO BAKE

Slice thinly 6 medium size unpeeled potatoes. Cover with water; let set 30 minutes. Drain.

Prepare casserole by spraying with Pam. Coat sides and bottom with dry crumbs. Layer potato slices and thinly sliced onions and salt. Top with a few crumbs.

Bake for 90 minutes at 350 degrees, covered; unmold.

POTATO CAKES

1	c. finely chopped onion	½	c. water
3	c. mashed or diced potatoes, cooked	½	tsp. garlic powder
		1	tsp. onion powder
3	c. bread crumbs		salt as needed

Mix well and spread thin on cookie sheet or as patties. Bake at 350 degrees until crisp.

POTATOES WITH TOMATO

Cook 3 pounds of potatoes. Mash the potatoes with 2 cups nut milk and onion salt and 3 tablespoons tomato puree. Serve.

POTATOES MASHED OR DICED

Add mashed carrots or rutabagas or finely shredded cabbage or spinach or corn, peas, chopped onion or blended fresh limas.

POTATO PATTIES

Cook 6 medium size cubed potatoes or equal amount of rice with 1 cup diced onion. Drain and partially mash. Add:

1½	c. drained corn	¼	tsp. garlic powder
¼	c. chopped parsley	½	tsp. onion powder
½	c. bread crumbs	1	tsp. vege salt

Form patties or spread thinly on cookie sheet.

Bake until brown and crisp.

POTATO SOUP (Cold Vichyssoise)

Cook:

1	c. chopped onions	4	c. water
4	c. sliced potatoes	3	Tbsp. chicken-flavored seasoning (McKay's)

Add 1¼ cups nut cream (½ cup raw cashews to 1 cup hot water). Blend all until creamy and refrigerate several hours.

Serve cold.

POTATO SOUP

Heat:

5	med. size diced, cooked potatoes	1	Tbsp. chicken-style seasoning (McKay's)
2	c. water	½	tsp. garlic salt

Blend until smooth:

1	Tbsp. dried onion	1	c. raw cashews
2	c. hot water	½	tsp. celery seed

Combine and heat and serve.

POTATOES STEWED

Cook until done:

1	lg. coarsely chopped onion	2½	c. water
		½	tsp. garlic salt
6	med. potatoes, cut in	¼	tsp. thyme
	½ inch slices	1	bay leaf (discard after cooking)

Add ½ cup chopped parsley after draining.
Serve.

SWEET POTATOES OR YAMS

A. Mash sweet potatoes. Top with thin orange slices and bake.
B. Layer 1 inch slices cooked sweet potatoes in a baking dish. Heat in saucepan 2 cups orange juice, 1 cup light or dark raisins and 2 tablespoons cornstarch. Cook to thicken. Remove from heat; add ½ cup walnuts and pour over potatoes. Heat, covered at 350 degrees for about 20 to 25 minutes.
C. Serve sweet potatoes or yams with hot applesauce.

POTATOES - SWEET OR YAMS

Lay 1 inch thick cooked yam slices and 1 inch raw apple slices, lightly salted, in casserole. Add crushed pineapple with juice.

Cover and cook until apples are done at 350 degrees.

SWEET POTATO FLUFF

3	med. size yams or sweet potatoes, cooked and mashed	1	8 oz. can crshd. pineapple
		½	c. sliced water chestnuts
		½	tsp. salt

Put in shallow baking dish topped with dry bread crumbs.
Bake at 350 degrees for 40 minutes.

SWEET POTATOES OR YAMS

Cook, skin and slice 6 medium size yams or sweet potatoes.

Combine in pan and cook until thickened:

1	c. orange juice grated rind from 1 orange	1	Tbsp. cornstarch

Pour sauce over yams in casserole.

Bake at 350 degrees for 45 minutes.

SAUERKRAUT STEW

1½	c. sauerkraut	1	tsp. caraway or dill seed
3	c. tomato juice, unsalted	6	med. potatoes, cut in 1 inch chunks

Cook until potatoes are done and serve.

SAUERKRAUT STUFFING

Mix well:

2	c. chopped onions, sauteed in ½ c. water	3	cooked grated potatoes
		1	tsp. dill seed
2	lbs. sauerkraut	2	slices bread, crumbled

Fill large, halved, seeded, but not peeled, zucchini squash.

Cook 45 minutes at 325 degrees.

TOMATOES

Dip tomato slices in seasoned bread crumbs and parsley and broil.

TOMATO - CASHEW SOUP

Combine 3 cups tomato juice or blended canned tomatoes with:

1	c. raw cashews, grd. fine	¼	tsp. garlic powder
1	tsp. onion powder	1	bay leaf (discard when cooked)

Heat well and serve.

TOMATO - CORN SOUP

Wash and core 3 pounds fresh tomatoes, chop. Cook in 1 pint of water for 10 minutes.

Cut kernels from 2 ears fresh corn and add ½ cup water, 1 bay leaf (discard after cooked), 1 pinch thyme, ¼ teaspoon marjoram, ¼ teaspoon basil, 1 tablespoon chicken-style seasoning (McKay's). Cook 7 minutes.

Put tomatoes through sieve and add to corn.

Simmer 10 minutes and serve.

TOMATO SOUP

Heat to boiling:

1	46 oz. can tomato juice	½	tsp. sweet basil
1	tsp. celery seed	¼	c. parsley
¼	c. lemon juice	¼	c. diced or grated onion
¼	tsp. cumin	1	Tbsp. soy sauce

For cream of tomato, add cashew cream; blend until smooth 2 cups hot water and 1 cup raw cashews.

TOMATO STEW

Cook:

6	med. potatoes, cubed	1	c. diced onions
2	c. water		

Add 2½ cups fresh or canned tomatoes, chopped.

TOMATO WHEAT

Combine cooked coarse cracked wheat, onion, tomato and parsley.

Serve hot or cold.

VITAMIN SOUP

Cook together until tender:

½	c. cabbage	1	c. sweet potato
½	c. carrots	½	c. onion
1	c. potatoes	½	c. celery
½	c. string beans	2	c. water

Add ½ cup tomatoes and salt. Blend 10 seconds. Add 1 cup cooked barley.

Heat and serve.

VEGETABLE COMBINATION

Combine and cook briefly:

1½	c. diagonally sliced carrots	1	c. slcd. mushrooms (opt.)
1½	c. sliced cauliflower	1	c. green limas
6	sliced green onions	1½	c. water
		3	Tbsp. soy sauce

Add 1 can whole green beans. May be slightly thickened.

Heat only; serve at once. Add almonds, if desired.

VEGETABLE GRAVY CASSEROLE

Layer in a casserole dish slices of cooked potatoes, slices of fresh tomatoes, whole cooked green beans, thinly sliced raw cabbage. Add thinly sliced raw onions. Pour over all a cashew gravy.

Bake at 350 degrees for 45 minutes.

ZUCCHINI

A. Very small zucchini are always best. Do not peel. Slice in half lengthwise. Sprinkle with herb salt. Use a mixture of onion, garlic and celery. Cook in small amount of water until barely done. They are delicious.

B. Cook coarsely grated zucchini, 1½ cups whole kernel corn with liquid, 1 small thinly sliced onion, and 2 large tomatoes, cut in wedges. Sprinkle with 1 teaspoon dill seed or 1 tablespoon freshly snipped dill.

C. Eat zucchini raw, too.

VEGETABLES MEXICAN

Cook 10 minutes:

½	c. water	1	c. chopped onion
1	c. finely sliced celery		

Add and cook 5 minutes:

2	c. canned corn w/liquid

Add and just heat:

2	c. fresh or canned tomatoes	1	c. fresh or canned sliced mushrooms (opt.)

132

| 1 | tsp. chicken-style seasoning (McKay's) | 1 | tsp. cumin |

VEGETABLES ON PASTA

Crisp cook:

1	c. slcd. mushrooms (opt.)	1	c. sliced carrots
1	c. sliced cauliflower	1	c. sliced zucchini
1	c. green peas	1	c. water

Blend:

| 1½ | c. hot water | ½ | c. raw cashews |
| 1 | tsp. chicken-style seasoning (McKay's) | | |

Add nut milk to the vegetables and serve over pasta or brown rice or barley.

ZUCCHINI CAULIFLOWER

Cook zucchini in 1 inch slices; cauliflower broken into small flowerettes.

Top with Avocado Dressing.

ZUCCHINI HERB CASSEROLE

Cook 7 minutes:

| 5 | c. zucchini, cubed | 1 | clove garlic, minced |
| 1 | c. sliced green onions | ¼ | c. water |

Add:

| 2 | tomatoes, peeled and chopped | ½ | tsp. ea. of basil and paprika and oregano |
| 1 | c. cooked brown rice | | |

Bake for 25 to 35 minutes in a 350 degree oven.

Vitamin B₁ (thiamine) aids in the release of energy from carbohydrates and helps in the synthesis of a nervous-system chemical. Found in lima beans, okra, onions, potatoes.

Vitamin B₂ (riboflavin) helps release energy from carbohydrates, proteins & fats, and helps in the maintenance of mucous membranes. Found in dried beans and peas, broccoli, collards, mushrooms, okra, winter squash.

Vitamin B₃ (niacin) works with B₁ and B₂ in producing energy in cells. Found in dried peas and beans, mushrooms, potatoes.

Vitamin C helps maintain capillaries, bones and teeth. Found in sweet peppers, potatoes, Brussels sprouts, tomatoes, broccoli, collards.

Vitamin E aids in the formation of red blood cells and muscle tissue and protects the body's source of vitamin A and C. Found in spinach, asparagus, broccoli leaves.

Calcium builds bones and teeth, helps maintain bone strength, aids in muscle contraction and blood clotting. Found in broccoli, collards, dandelion greens.

Potassium aids muscle contraction, transmission of nerve impulses and the release of energy from carbohydrates, proteins and fats. Found in potatoes, squash, dried peas and beans.

Iron keeps red blood cells healthy. Found in lima beans, broccoli, spinach, potatoes.

RECIPE INDEX

BREADS

FOREIGN-STYLE FOODS

FRUITS

GRAVIES

JAMS AND FRUIT RELISHES

MAIN DISHES

SALAD DRESSINGS

SAUCES

VEGETABLES

ALPHABETICAL INDEX *

* Prepared by Fannie L. Houck

This Book and Other Fine Publications are Available From:

M M I Press
Aldworth Road
P.O. Box 279
Harrisville, NH 03450
(603) 827-3769